GOD'S BUSINESS PLAN

GOD'S BUSINESS PLAN

TERRY STEPHENS II

Copyright © 2017 Terry W. Stephens II

T & W Publishing

www.manifestationchurch.com
info@manifestationchurch.com

All rights reserved. Written permission must be secured from the publisher to use or reproduce any part of this book, except for brief quotations in critical reviews or articles.

ISBN-13: 978-0-9852631-2-6 (Paperback)
ISBN-13: 978-0-9852631-3-3 (eBook)

Book Title: God's Business Plan
Author: Terry Stephens II
Editing: David Clarke - Clarke Columbus Consultant

ACKNOWLEDGMENTS

It is with great pleasure that I give thanks to the many preachers, teachers, authors, and mentors that have inspired me in so many different ways.

Thank you to my wife, Janet, and our children - your sacrifice has not gone unnoticed.

Thank you to the men of God that have cared for my soul over the years: My former pastor while serving in the Army in Germany, Pastor Arlee Robinson, Apostle Phillip Byler my former pastor while serving in Ft. Stewart, GA, who was instrumental in my introduction to the ministry.

Thanks to my Aunt Jackie Sims who has always been a steady sounding board from whom I have learned so much. To the greatest church in the world, Manifestation Church, who is structured in the manner this book outlines, I love you and am honored to worship with you.

Thanks to my uncle Dale Stephens, such a prolific teacher and student of the word.

To my grandmother Betty Stephens, my biggest fan, who prayed for me unconditionally. So many prophetic words have come to me confirming your prayers for me. Life is not the same without you. RIH. Thank you for being a prayer warrior on my behalf.

Special thanks to my Apostle, Lafayette Scales. I've searched far and wide looking to find the fivefold ministry operating in harmony in a local church. I found that and more at Rhema Christian Center. Thank you for your love and example.

To my parents, Terry and Teresa Stephens - to whom I owe the greatest debt because of their deposit of a great spiritual upbringing. You are both my natural and spiritual parents and I thank you so much for teaching me how to connect with a holy God.

To my Jesus, the alpha and omega - without you this book would not be possible. Without you I don't know where I would be. I thank you for never giving up on me and trusting me with the care of your word. Thank you.

This book is dedicated to my father, a man who was thirty years ahead of his time. Much of what's going on in the body of Christ today, my father was talking about thirty years before. Of course, he was in an environment that didn't believe in the fivefold ministry and spiritual gifts. Although many of his contemporaries didn't listen to him, I am so glad I did.

This book is also dedicated to my kids Janeyce, Janique, Tre, Jaylin, Andre, and Maya. Everything I do is motivated by my love for you.

I love you guys.

CONTENTS

Introduction	xi
1. Team Ministry in the Kingdom	1
2. Prophet Priest King	5
3. Adam Needs an Example of Leadership	17
4. The Supernatural in Action	21
5. Evangelism - Brazen Altar Ministry (Be Fruitful)	39
6. Teaching - Brazen Laver (Multiply)	63
7. Pastor - Table of Shewbread (Replenish the Earth)	75
8. Prophecy - Golden Candlesticks (Subdue)	87
9. Apostle - Altar of Incense (Have Dominion)	99
10. The Fivefold Ministry & The Tabernacle	107
11. Wisdom for Governing the Fivefold Ministry	125
References	135
About the Author	137

INTRODUCTION

There are many people in our world today who endeavor to lead others to accomplish certain goals. We have learned many things from the Bible and we have learned many things from the experiences of others. The more I travel and watch leaders, the more I realize that many of us are simply doing what we saw others do. Although some things others have done while relying on their own intelligence may have achieved the results that were intended, in order to be most effective, we must always use the word of God as our motivation for why and how we lead people. Leadership has always been a core part of the plan for the advancement of the Kingdom of God and we've learned many principles of leadership from leaders in the Bible. Men such as Moses, Joseph, David, Paul, and many others have all given us great examples of leadership.

In this book as the Spirit of God illuminates my mind, I plan to present a process Jesus used in his task of establishing the Kingdom of Heaven on earth. I pray that you understand these principles so that you may have clear instructions on how to lead the people that God has given you. This book has a two-fold application. The first being the how-to process of leadership using the fivefold ministry gifts and how they were meant to work as a team, the other being developing the leadership structure of the local church. I plan to show that these fivefold ministry gifts or five ascension gifts as mentioned by others, were never intended to operate as "lone rangers." They were meant to work as a team - each gift with special abilities in certain areas to give the body of Christ the necessary ingredients for proper growth and maturity. The lone ranger ministry has not worked and is stunting the growth of the people of God. In essence, what you will find in this book is God's business plan. A detailed look at how God plans to achieve his goals for the Kingdom. I pray that this book helps the body to make the proper adjustments necessary for the sake of the Kingdom.

1

TEAM MINISTRY IN THE KINGDOM
(FAMILY FOUNDATION)

The lone ranger ministry model must end. It is obvious the lone ranger mentality and way of ministry is not working and is in desperate need of reformation. Nowhere in scripture do we see that the body of Christ was to be perfected and matured by one person. Not even Jesus operated by himself. Even Jesus the prophet, priest and king built a team of disciples to help him establish and continue the Kingdom. Even Jesus had a prophet, John the Baptist, who prepared the way for his ministry. Team ministry has been around ever since the Garden of Eden, where the leadership team consisted of God, Adam and Eve. The family was the first institution God established in the earth. Establishing a strong family foundation was chief building block to God's plan for his Kingdom. God put a man and woman in a structured garden with specific instructions. *Then God said, "Let us make mankind in our image, in our likeness, so that they may rule over the fish in the sea and the birds in the sky, over*

the livestock and all the wild animals, and over all the creatures that move along the ground." So God created mankind in his own image, in the image of God he created them; male and female he created them. God blessed them and said to them, "Be fruitful and increase in number; fill the earth and subdue it. Rule over the fish in the sea and

the birds in the sky and over every living creature that moves on the ground." (Genesis 1:26-28) NIV

There's so much to point out here but for now we'll deal with the fact that God blesses man first, which means that he empowered them. And when you understand the details of the fall which we will deal with later, you'll understand how significant the Holy Spirit is to us. But what I want to point out here is that God gave Adam and Eve and fivefold mandate.

Be fruitful

Multiply

Replenish the earth

Subdue

Have dominion

These five instructions represent God's plan for our families. These instructions exemplify the goal of build, maintain, and advance the family.

Before we go further into the fivefold mandate, let's look at the structure of the family. According to Genesis we see a threefold foundational leadership structure. God, Adam, and Eve. They represent the Prophet, Priest, and King model that is seen throughout the Old and New testament as God's foundational leadership structure. God as King, Adam as the Prophet, and Eve as the Priest. Look at the way God structured the family and eventually the leadership of the children of Israel as they became a nation throughout the whole Old Testament.

2

PROPHET PRIEST KING

Prophet	Priest	King
Adam	Eve	God
Moses	Aaron	God
Samuel	Ahimelech	Saul
Samuel/Nathan	Zadok	David
Nathan	Azariah	Solomon

Just to name a few.

So team ministry began with the family foundation. God with Adam and Eve, in a structured garden, fulfilling specific instructions - a fivefold mandate. Team ministry has and always will be the standard. We see this structure and fivefold mandate in the New Testament as well. We will go into further detail later in this book.

In Ephesians chapter 4:11-13 the bible says "It was he who gave some to be apostles, some to be prophets, some to be evangelists, and some to be pastors and teachers to prepare God's people for works of service, so that the body of Christ may be built up until we all reach unity in the faith and in the knowledge of the Son of God and become mature, attaining to the whole measure of the fullness of Christ." (NIV) I have a question. Where in these passages does it suggests that these gifted men and women are to start local churches and only expose their particular part of the body to one of the gifts, which happens to be the one in which they operate? Honestly, I don't see that anywhere in the Bible, nor does scripture suggest it. The fivefold ministry gifts or five ascension gifts were given to us as a team of gifts that serve a specific function to aid the body of Christ in achieving wholeness and maturity in a local church context. Because the book of Ephesians was written to a specific local church, I believe that as the scripture says some to be, it means some of every gift in local churches. Just like a business may have an accounting department, I believe that every local church should have departments with some evangelists functioning in the capacity of evangelists, some teachers functioning as teachers, some pastors functioning as pastors, etc. Many compare the fivefold ministry to the hand. Others compare them to the five food groups. I like to refer to them as the meat and potatoes to God's business plan. However, you look at them the key is understanding that they all are powerful individually but achieve more together.

I believe that all five gifts should be in operation in every local church, every organization, every denomination, and every fellowship. I believe this because God's original intent was never to have a bunch of churches, denominations, fellowships, etc., that all operated, believed, and lived differently. God's original intent was to have a Kingdom on the earth that he would rule over through the spirits of men. With the Kingdom mindset, we understand that Kingdoms don't expand or advance by individual aspiration. Kingdoms advance through colonization. Colonization is the extension of political and economic control over an area by a state whose nationals have occupied the area and usually possess organizational or technological superiority over the native population. It may consist simply of a migration of nationals to the territory, or it may be the formal assumption of control over the territory by military or civil representatives of the dominant power. The term is also applied to a group of nationals who settle in a foreign country or territory but retain political or cultural connections with their parent state.

Overpopulation, economic distress, social unrest, and religious persecution in the home country may be factors that lead to colonization. But, colonization is mostly the result of imperialism, which is the extension of rule or influence by one government, nation, or society over another. Colonization may be state policy, or it may be a private project sponsored by chartered corporations or by associations and individuals. Before colonization can be achieved, the indigenous population must be subdued and assimilated or converted to the culture of the colonists - otherwise, a modus vivendi must be established by the imposition of a treaty or an alliance.

Colonialism is also the establishment, maintenance, acquisition and expansion of colonies in one territory by people from another territory. It is a process whereby sovereignty over the colony is claimed by the metropole "mother city or country" and the social structure, government, and economics of the colony are changed by colonists - people from the metropole.

When speaking in terms of colonization, I'm not referring to legalism and tradition. I'm suggesting that God fully intended for the kingdom to operate and function like a kingdom governmentally, economically, and socially.

The bible says in Ephesians 2:19, 20, "Consequently, you are no longer foreigners and aliens, but fellow citizens with God's people and members of God's household, built on the foundation of the apostles and prophets, with Christ Jesus himself as the chief cornerstone." (NIV)

Paul here is talking about God's people, the church, kingdom citizens, the ecclesia, the called out ones. He says that the Church is built on the foundation of the apostles and prophets with Jesus Christ as the chief cornerstone. This represents the functions of Jesus as Prophet, Priest, and King. In the Old Testament we find three main offices that functioned in leadership over the Children of

Israel - God's Kingdom. According to scripture, when speaking of the Tabernacle of Moses, there were two sets of leadership among the Children of Israel. The first is what I call the "foundational leadership," made up the offices of the Prophet, Priest, and King. The second is what I call the "ministry leadership," which was made up of the Levitical priesthood, which is represented in our time by the fivefold ministry gifts.

God established the prophet and priest early in the wilderness after Israel's exodus from Egypt. Moses served as the prophet and Aaron as the priest. During this time, God was and still is King. But as time went by, the people began to request a human king (I Samuel 8). God gave them Saul, then David, etc. Throughout the Old Testament, when Israel wasn't in bondage, they had these three offices serving in these distinct capacities. The prophet revealed God, spoke for God, and declared the truths of God (Luke 13:33). The priest was to bore the sins of the people and made intercession for their transgressions (Hebrews 9:26-27). The king ruled, judged and protected the citizens of the kingdom (Matthew 27:11). In this time (post Jesus time), the foundation of our churches should be from the ministry of the apostles and prophets working together as directed by the Holy Spirit, the chief cornerstone. A healthy church needs the Prophets to enlighten us through revelatory speaking for God, Priests (Holy Spirit) to lead us to God for relationship with God and Kings (apostles) to administrate and enforce the task and mission of God. You see in the Old Testament, once God delivered the children of Israel out of Egypt, he began to set them up as a kingdom that he would Lord over as King. He began by establishing the leadership with Moses and Aaron as the leaders. Again Moses as the Prophet, Aaron as the Priest and God was, is, and always will be King.

Over time, as Samuel was instructed to anoint Saul as King, the triune leadership structure now filled all offices with a human being. Although this was not God's original intent, God was gracious enough to grant the children of Israel their request. So, in the Old Testament God, Moses, and Aaron fulfilled the offices of Prophet, Priest, and King.

In the New Testament, Jesus fulfilled all three offices during his ministry on the earth. Now, in the post Jesus era, the offices are filled by the apostles in the role or function as kings, prophets as prophets and the Holy Spirit as Jesus, the chief cornerstone (Ephesians 2:20 NIV). This is the structure of foundational government set for the church. The prophet, priest, and king ministries are the foundational ministries of the church.

It is my opinion that when Jesus sent the disciples out to minister two by two in the gospels, he was establishing another structure principle for ministry - so when the Holy Ghost came he (the Holy Ghost) would complete the trilogy. "Two people are better off than one, for they can help each other succeed" Ecclesiastes 4:9 (NLT). We also see this again after Jesus' death, resurrection, and ascension. "While they were worshiping the Lord and fasting, the Holy Spirit said, "Set apart for me Barnabas and Saul for the work to which I have called them." So after they had fasted and prayed, they placed their hands on them and sent them off." (Acts 13:2, 3 NIV). This principle of two is all over the bible. "Calling the Twelve to him, he sent them out two by two and gave them authority over evil spirits" (Mark 6:7 NIV). Why the principle of two? He set up the principle of two so that when the Holy Ghost came, he (the Holy Ghost) would complete the trilogy. God has always worked in three's as well, making Himself the center of all we do God understands that two is the number of division or separation. The Son who has two natures: human and divine. There are 2 Testaments: the Old and New. Mankind is Male and Female. Romans 9 speaks of two vessels - one for honorable use and the other for dishonorable use. There are two types of people - sheep and goats. There are two ages, this age and the age to come: Matt. 12:32; 13:39, 40, 49; Mark 10:30. Two plus Him make three and now there's no division or separation.

Now three is the number of perfection. The Trinity consists of Father, Son, and Holy Spirit. There are three qualities of the universe: Time, Space, and Matter. To exist (except for God), all three are required. Each quality consists of three elements. Therefore, we live in a trinity of trinities. Jesus functioned as Prophet, Priest, and King.

The three qualities of the universe are each three:

Time is one yet three. Space is one yet three. Matter is one yet three:

Past	Height	Solid
Present	Width	Liquid
Future	Depth	Gas

Man is made of three - body, soul, and Spirit. Human abilities are three - thought, word, and deed. Why a threefold foundation? "And though a man might prevail against him who is alone, two will withstand him. A threefold cord is not quickly broken" (Ecclesiastes 4:12 AMP). The apostle, prophet, and Holy Spirit working in harmony together is a foundation that is not quickly broken. If your church is not built on this foundation, then I urge you to ask God for wisdom to transition to his model. This is not new. The Tabernacle of Moses was built on this foundation as well, which, I believe is a picture of the Kingdom structure, a local church model, as well as the many other shadows and types it represents. The Tabernacle is

God's expression of church. It was a picture of how we are to do church. Away with this Babylonian model of church that was instituted by Constantine. Constantine and the Roman Catholic church never had and still don't embrace the Truth of Jesus Christ as Lord and King. In order for the body of Christ to achieve the goals of the Kingdom set forth by God we must do away with the worldly systems we've embraced and truly seek first the kingdom and his righteousness. Seeking the kingdom isn't just about achieving the goals of the kingdom, but also achieving those goals in the way that he has prescribed they be achieved. We must seek his way of doing things. The Tabernacle is not only our example as to how to do church but also is type and shadow of the process to spiritual maturity. All throughout the bible God is showing us his business plan. From the garden of Eden to the Tabernacle of Moses to Solomon's Temple, even in the Old Testament prophetic books and the Gospels. It's time for the body of Christ to learn his plan and follow it, in order to achieve God results.

3

ADAM NEEDS AN EXAMPLE OF LEADERSHIP

Before we talk about God's business plan and the process to spiritual maturity, we must understand certain things that took place before the arrival of Jesus. In Genesis chapter one, the chapter of creation, we find everything our amazing God has created and the purposes for which they were created. It's very important to understand God's reason for creating the earth and man and interesting to see how God chose to create them.

Genesis chapter one is the foundation of everything we deal with in life. There are many lessons we can learn about God in this chapter that help us as leaders, husbands, managers, etc. One lesson we must understand is everything created was brought into existence by God's word. John 1:1 says, "In the beginning was the Word, and the Word was with God, and the Word was God."

God's word is so important because it is the source from which we all have come. There is much to learn from the fact that God created the Heavens and the Earth through his word. In Genesis chapter one, God took six days creating them both by speaking what He wanted into existence. On the seventh day He rested from work. This tells us communication is a big part of leadership. A leader must be able to effectively communicate what he wants in order for his vision to come to pass. God took six days to communicate and decree his vision. "Death and life are in the power of the tongue: and they that love it shall eat the fruit thereof" (Proverbs 18:21).

The number six is the number for man, because God created man on the sixth day. The number six also represents human labor. Today, working six days and resting on the seventh (or keeping the Sabbath as we learn in the Book of Moses) has become a universal practice around the world. This example is also key in how we as kingdom citizens operate even now in the kingdom. This is the process of creation. The number six represents natural labor and the number seven represents completion or fulfillment. Working six days and resting on the seventh day represents man's natural labor and God completing the work. The only difference is, God is divine and doesn't need labor. He speaks and it manifests.

Man must work in the supernatural, where God puts his divinity on our natural labor - but nothing happens unless voice has been given to it. When we give voice to the word of God, we give the angels permission and orders to carry out on our behalf. "Bless the LORD, ye his angels, that excel in strength, that do his commandments, hearkening unto the voice of his word" (Psalms 103:20).

4

THE SUPERNATURAL IN ACTION

Friends the supernatural is critical for authentic ministry. We've learned by now that entertainment alone isn't working we need the real power of God. For example, Joshua used the same process while following God's instructions during the battle of Jericho. In Joshua chapter six, God told Joshua and the children of Israel to march around the city of Jericho one time for six days.

> *"You shall march around the enclosure, all the men of war going around the city once. This you shall do for six days.*
>
> *And seven priests shall bear before the ark seven trumpets of rams' horns; and on the seventh day you*

shall march around the enclosure seven times, and the priests shall blow the trumpets. When they make a long blast with the ram's horn and you hear the sound of the trumpet, all the people shall shout with a great shout; and the wall of the enclosure shall fall down in its place and the people shall go up [over it], every man straight before him"

— *JOSHUA 6:3-5 AMP*

Now, what we must understand as leaders is God is *divine* - He is a deity. So yes, while God can create with only His words, we as human beings are *not* divine and we must operate in the supernatural. The supernatural is God putting His divine efforts on our natural labor. This is what we see in this passage of scripture, which serves as a prime example of the supernatural in action.

Joshua and the children of Israel marched around the walls of Jericho once a day, for six days as God instructed. This represents the natural labor needed for the supernatural to take place. Then, the seven priests with seven trumpets of ram's horns marched around Jericho seven times on the seventh day and they blew the trumpets.

Seven is the number of completion or spiritual perfection. There are seven days of the week. There are seven colors (red, orange, yellow, green, blue, indigo and violet) in the visible light spectrum. There are seven seals, seven trumpets, seven parables in Matthew, and seven promises to the church. Seven represents God putting His "super" on your "natural."

So on the seventh day, when the children of Israel heard the seven trumpets sound, they shouted a great shout. Here we see how the supernatural operates with a combination of natural and divine. The people of Israel had to shout because, as we saw in Genesis one, the divine works by voice.

This principle concerning the supernatural is in motion throughout the bible. Look at what they said about Jesus. *"What things?" he asked. "About Jesus of Nazareth," they replied. "He was a prophet, powerful in word and deed before God and all the people"* (Luke 24:19 NIV). Even Jesus had to operate within the principle of the supernatural. Consequently, if one endeavors to lead in the Kingdom of God, one must operate in the supernatural.

But now, we must understand the reason things changed and why Jesus was sent to show us how to lead. Genesis 1:26- 28 reads, "And God said, Let us make man in our image, after our likeness: and let them have dominion over the fish of the sea, and over the fowl of the air, and over the cattle, and over all the earth, and over every creeping thing that creepeth upon the earth. So God created man in his own image, in the image of God created he him; male and female created he them. And God blessed them, and God said unto them, Be fruitful, and multiply, and replenish the earth, and subdue it: and have dominion over the fish of the sea, and over the fowl of the air, and over every living thing that moveth upon the earth".

Man was made in the image of God for a reason. It's the image of God that gives the Kingdom its identity. Everything in the Kingdom should bear this image. Just like a product from companies all bear a certain seal that identifies them as belonging or made by a certain company. So are we the workmanship of Christ, bearing the seal of his image.

> *Nevertheless the foundation of God standeth sure, having this seal, The Lord knoweth them that are his. And, Let every one that nameth the name of Christ depart from iniquity.*

— *2 TIMOTHY 2:19*

What is that seal? It is the seal of the DNA of Christ, the image of God. Watch what 2 Corinthians 4:4 says,

> *In whom the god of this world hath blinded the minds of them which believe not, lest the light of the glorious gospel of Christ, who is the image of God, should shine unto them.*

> *Who being the brightness of his glory, and the express image of his person, and upholding all things by the word of his power, when he had by himself purged our sins, sat down on the right hand of the Majesty on high;*

— *HEBREWS 1:3 KJV*

In these passages of scripture, we find that mankind was not only created to be in God's family, but also to execute the fivefold mandate. Mankind was to do it in a specific way that would give God glory. Bearing God's image is what gives God glory. His image is what magnifies and shines a light on him and his power.

1 Corinthians 11:7 says "For a man indeed ought not to cover his head, forasmuch as he is the image and glory of God: but the woman is the glory of the man." When we walk according to the image we were made to be, we shine a light that gives glory to God.

> *For whom he did foreknow, he also did predestinate to be conformed to the image of his Son, that he might be the firstborn among many brethren.*
>
> — ROMANS 8:29

Friends we weren't predestined to be doctors, lawyers, athletes, and politicians. We were predestined to be conformed to the image of God. These professions and the things we do are just different avenues in which that image is expressed. Mankind was made for leadership. It was God's intention for man to rule over the earth and have dominion. Webster's dictionary defines dominion as "control or exercising control of; sovereignty. Man was to control or exercise control over the earth and every living thing that moved upon the earth. Man was to be fruitful, to produce in abundance; multiply, replenish the earth, subdue, conquer and subjugate and have dominion. This was mankind's mission, his purpose, his destiny - his reason for being. God has not made covenant with any person, place, or thing without giving them a job to do. Adam, Abraham, Noah, David, Elijah, Paul, John the Baptist - all had a job to do. The animals have purpose as well. The water has purpose. The moon and sun have purpose. Natural resources like oil, coal, gold, iron, etc., all have purpose. So, man's purpose was leadership. Genesis Ch. 2:18 God realizes that man was going to need help. So, He first inventories the rest of his living creations to see if any of the animals can do the job. When Adam finds no suitable help meet among the animals, God then makes the woman out of the side of the man. The woman's purpose according to verse 18 in Genesis Ch. 2 is to be a helpmeet, or a helper. So what is she to help with? She is to help with the mission that God had given Adam. Every man of God should have a mission from God. Otherwise when he chooses a wife, she will be very confused and frustrated, because she was made to help. If the man has no mission, then she is not able to operate in her purpose. When the purpose of a thing is not known, then abuse is sure to follow (Myles Munroe). A part of man's leadership was to ensure everything under his dominion was fulfilling its purpose. The reason for many failed marriages is husbands and wives have been trying to use each other for the wrong purpose. Simply put, marriage is two people coming into covenant together in order to accomplish the vision God has given them. That's why the bible says in Proverbs 18:22, "The man who finds a wife finds a treasure, and he receives favor from the Lord" (NLT). In order for a man to accomplish his mission, he is going to need help. The woman is the help he needs and the skills and abilities she brings to him will be as favor from the Lord.

Adam failed in his leadership concerning his wife, Eve. How did Adam fail in leadership concerning Eve? Adam failed in the area of setting the example. I truly believe that had Adam not agreed to take part in eating of the tree, that the punishment, for Eve only, would not have been as severe. Neither would we in generations to come be suffering from her error. The instructions were given to Adam alone. Although Eve knew that she wasn't to eat of the tree. Eve wasn't the one responsible, Adam was. But before we indict Adam with total responsibility let's examine one more thing - Adam hadn't been taught to lead. Adam had never dealt with disobedience before this incident. He himself had never been disobedient before, so, this was new to him. God had dealt with disobedience before, with Satan.

We see a pattern with God and disobedience. God is not like man that puts measures in place to keep others from disobedience. God, like he did with Satan, will allow choice to take full course and reward and consequence are the results of that choice. Again, because Adam was innocent and had never dealt with disobedience, he didn't know how to properly lead in this situation. Now Adam is stuck with the results of their agreed upon disobedience. They are separated from God and Adam still has no example of how to properly lead in a new environment where disobedience is becoming the norm. But God, the great redeemer, always has a plan of redemption. And God announces his redemption plan as he administers punishment to the parties involved in the disobedience. That redemption plan is Jesus Christ. Every good leader should always have a backup plan. But Jesus was not just God's redemption plan - He was now mankind's' example of leadership. He was to demonstrate, teach, and activate mankind into continuing the mission under the present and future circumstances.

I Corinthians 11:3 says "But I would have you know, that the head of every man is Christ; and the head of the woman is the man; and the head of Christ is God". (KJV) This scripture is explaining to all parties who they should look to for an example of leadership. Christ, meaning Jesus the anointed one, was to be the example of leadership to man. Man was to be the example of leadership to the woman. And God was the example of leadership to Jesus, the anointed one.

That's why the bible tells us in Ephesians 5:23 "For the husband is the head of the wife, even as Christ is the head of the church; and he is the savior of the body." I truly believe that just as Jesus is our savior, past, present, and future through his shedding of blood for our sins, Adam could have saved mankind from the curse of sin and death had he stood in his place of leadership and set the example of obedience.

All the characters mentioned in these passages, Christ, man, and woman have something in common. They all must submit their lives in obedience to another one in authority. Christ submits to God, man submits to Christ, and the woman submits to man. Each knows what it's like to depend on someone else for leadership, provision, access, protection, etc. The bible says in Hebrews 4:15 "For we have not an high priest that cannot be touched with the feeling of our infirmities; but was in all points tempted like as we are, yet without sin". (KJV) The best leaders, husbands, parents, supervisors, etc., are those that can sympathize with the issues of their subordinates.

Jesus being tempted by Satan in the book of Matthew is an example of how to deal with temptation. This is what this book is about - Adam needed an example of leadership and Jesus has come to be our example. Not only did Adam need an example of leadership, but he needed an example of protection. Adam didn't understand that with the addition of Eve his responsibility of leader was not only to provide vision and direction, but protection as well.

The bible says in Matthew 12:29 "Or else how can one enter into a strong man's house, and spoil his goods, except he first bind the strong man? And then he will spoil his house". Satan understood this scripture way back in the beginning with Adam and Eve. He understood that in order to defeat Adam he had to defeat the strong man. What was the strong man? The strong man was the fortress of belief that if they ate of the tree of the knowledge of good and evil, they would die and also become like God. Whoever or whatever you believe in is the strong man in your life. So as we see in Genesis Chapter 2, Satan through lies and deceit defeats Adam and Eve by making them believe his lies. Because Adam and Eve believed Satan, they became servant to him. Not only did God's word come true and they experienced spiritual death, but now they became slaves to Satan. That's why the scripture tells us we were all born in sin and shaped in iniquity. Because now, the authority mankind once had was taken through deceit and is in the hands of Satan. No wonder the bible refers to Satan as the thief. "The thief cometh not, but for to steal, and to kill, and to destroy: I am come that they might have life, and that they may have it more abundantly" (John 10:10). Because he tricked them, even though they knew they were not to eat the fruit of the tree, Satan still is guilty of theft in the eyes of God.

Another area Adam needed an example with was protecting his house. With one sin, Adam lost his authority and his house.

So now because of this failure in leadership, Jesus comes to restore all things and be an example to us on the who, what, when, where, and how's of leadership. Jesus was a wise leader, whose every move was on purpose.

For example, let's talk about James and John. The Bible tells us James and John were very successful fishermen. They were not people who were doing nothing with their lives, just hoping for prosperity to overtake them out of the sky. They were hard working, committed, and very skilled in their craft. That explains the "who" aspect. If I saw these men I would choose them to be on my team as well. There is no place for laziness in the Kingdom of God. God will always choose the one who is working over the lazy bum. Why? Because in order for the supernatural to manifest, there must be some work, labor, and toil in the earth realm.

Well, what was his plan for James and John? The bible says that Jesus planned to make them fishers of men. You see, Jesus understood their skill in fishing could be used in the kingdom as well. Jesus was not about to take these men out of their element. He needed people who knew how to gather other people. A man that understands the principles of fishing should be able to understand fishing for people as well. A kingdom is no good without people.

Thirdly, he knew when to go after them. In Luke Chapter 5, Jesus waited until they were struggling with their fishing to evangelize them. He understood when things are going great it's hard to get people to change, <u>but failure can be a motivator for change</u>. Fourthly, Jesus was in the right place at the right time. You can't evangelize people from where you are. You have got to go where they are. Being in the right place was also important to the method of evangelism that he would use. Finally, he understood how to get them. People are drawn by success. If you are successful in an area that I'm lacking in, then I'm all ears, because I need what you have. Jesus showed himself worthy to be their leader; He could do what they couldn't. Just think about it. Why do people go to the hospital? Because the hospital can do what people can't do for themselves. We as the people of God must tap into the power and authority that God has given us in order to provide for the needs of the people. As a result of providing for their needs, we are able to attract citizens for the kingdom. Why do people from all over the world apply for Visa's to come to America? Simply put, we have something that they can't get for themselves where they are.

So how did Jesus lead? Was there a specific method or pattern that he used? Did he use certain tools or gifts that we can use in order to have the effectiveness that he did? It is my belief that not only did Jesus function in the offices of Prophet, Priest, and King during his ministry on the earth, but he also used the fivefold ministry gifts written of in Ephesians 4, in a specific pattern in order to achieve maturity in his disciples. Jesus also used many of the other gifts noted in I Corinthians 12 and Romans 12. I believe that Jesus understood the fivefold ministry gifts would be critical to the colonization and advancement of the Kingdom. He understood that each function served as a key element in the development and maturing of the saints. Without one, the health of the body of Christ would suffer greatly. Lack is something every father or King despises when it comes to those they love. Jesus also understood the importance of these gifts working together in harmony, with the understanding that God's original intent was to have a Kingdom on the earth, administrated and expanded by mankind. These fivefold ministry gifts were given for the purpose of advancing the Kingdom. But we've messed up because we haven't used these gifts properly. These gifts or gifted men and women were meant to work together. They are the details to God's business plan to build, maintain, and advance the Kingdom of God. Consider these examples of God business structure and process seen throughout the bible in effort to advance the Kingdom.

God's Business plan

Prophet + Priest + King

Adam + Eve + God

1. Be fruitful
2. Multiply
3. Replenish the earth
4. Subdue it
5. Have dominion

Prophet + Priest + King

Moses + Aaron + God

1. Brazen Altar
2. Brazen Lavar
3. Table of Showbread
4. Golden Candlesticks
5. Altar of Incense

Prophet + Priest + King

Nathan + Zadok + David

1. Brazen Altar
2. Brazen Lavar
3. Table of Showbread
4. Golden Candlesticks
5. Altar of Incense

Prophet + Priest + King

Prophet + Jesus + Apostle

1. Evangelists
2. Teacher
3. Pastor
4. Prophet
5. Apostle

Let's think of it in terms of seed.

The evangelist gathers and puts the seed in the soil.

The teacher washes or fertilizes the seed.

The pastor puts the fruit in the right environment.

The prophet declares when the fruit is to be plucked.

The apostle distributes the fruit.

Each one of the fivefold ministry gifts has a specific function and is vital to the growth and development of the seed maturing to fruitfulness. It was God's intent that these gifted men and women would work together for the perfecting of the saints. I can just imagine how healthy our bodies would be if we only ate meat. We would all be a part of the obesity population, which by the way is growing more and more dangerous as time goes by. Hmmm, I would dare to say that obesity is going on in the body of Christ as well. Ok, by now you should get the point. Every local church needs to have all five of the gifts functioning in order for those kingdom citizens to grow to be healthy and mature as well so that those converted can be properly matured and trained in doing the work of the ministry.

Considers the following as God's business plan

Church	Tabernacle	Garden	Business
Evangelists	Brazen Altar	Be Fruitful	Recruiters
Teachers	Brazen Lavar	Multiply	Trainers
Pastors	Table of Shewbread	Replenish	Supervisor
Prophets	Golden Candlesticks	Subdue	Advisors
Apostles	Altar of Incense	Dominion	Administrators

These gifts don't define who a person is, they define the area in which a person functions on the team.

5

EVANGELISM - BRAZEN ALTAR MINISTRY (BE FRUITFUL)

(RECRUITING AND MARKETING)

Evangelism is the art of preaching the gospel to unbelievers. Many who feel the call to evangelism hold Matthew 28:19, 20 very near and dear to their heart. Evangelism has a very broad function within the fivefold ministry. Evangelists have the responsibility of converting new citizens to the Kingdom of God through the good news. Jesus told the disciples in Matthew 10 to preach the Kingdom, heal the sick, raise the dead, cleanse the lepers, and drive out demons. So as you can see, the ministry of an evangelist is not just going around preaching from church to church. Nor is it reserved just for women. Evangelists are known as the gatherers. They excel in gathering large crowds of people for the cause of Christ. Their responsibility is bringing people to and through the born again process, which we call the death, burial, and resurrection. I know that many teach that all you have to do is confess with your mouth and believe with your heart and you are saved - but that is not correct. The scripture says that you shall be saved after you have confessed with your mouth and believed in your heart. "That if you shall confess with your mouth the Lord Jesus, and shall believe in your heart that God has raised him from the dead, you shall be saved" (Romans 10:9). The word shall indicate a promise or oath. Confessing with your mouth and believing with your heart is like accepting a marriage invitation. You intend to get married, but you are not married yet. The born again process is much like getting married. Both parties must consent to this binding covenant. Jesus committed to us through Calvary, his death, burial, and resurrection. So, just like in a natural marriage, where both parties must say I do, spiritually we must go through our own death, burial, and resurrection. "And he that taketh not his cross, and followeth after me, is not worthy of me" (Matthew 10:38). The way we consent to covenant with God is through our own death, burial, and resurrection called repentance, baptism, and receiving the Holy Ghost according to Acts 2:38.

Consider this comparison:

Death	Burial	Resurrection
Repentance	Baptism	Holy Spirit
Engagement	Ceremony	Honeymoon

"Then Peter said unto them, Repent, and be baptized every one of you in the name of Jesus Christ for the remission of sins, and ye shall receive the gift of the Holy Ghost" (Acts 2:38). When dealing with repentance, we must understand that Adam and Eve's sin separated us from God. So, we (mankind) at one time were in covenant with God. So "re-," a prefix, occurring originally in loanwords from Latin, is used with the meaning "again" or "again and again" to indicate repetition, or with the meaning "back" or "backward" to indicate withdrawal or backward motion. And "-pent" means "kept in, or confined". When we put the two together we get, to confine again or to commit again. Repentance is all about returning back to God. Recognizing that your time in sin and covenant with Satan is not what you want.

Repentance is the engagement process. "If my people who are called by my name shall humble themselves, pray, and seek my face, and turn from their wicked ways; then will I hear from heaven, and forgive their sin, and will heal their land" (II Chronicles 7:14 KJV).

Repentance gets you back in right standing with God much like an engagement is meant to get you ready for your life with your mate.

Now the baptism part is really very simple. God wants us to openly and without shame commit to him. So, he uses baptism as a ceremony, so that everyone will know that we are his. In the Old Testament, whenever a covenant was conducted, it was always by a ceremony. Without repentance, water baptism is merely an empty symbol. But with repentance, water baptism remits sins. When traveling to different countries there are certain things the governments of these countries won't allow you to bring with you when crossing their borders. Well, Jesus the King will not allow sin in his kingdom. Jesus connected repentance with remission of sins in His final instructions to His disciples in Luke 24:47. "And that repentance and remission of sins should be preached in his name among all nations, beginning at Jerusalem". Baptism is the means by which we leave our sins behind, thus removing any condemnation. Therefore, we are buried with him by baptism into death: that like as Christ was raised up from the dead by the glory of the Father, even so we also should walk in newness of life. (Romans 6:4, 5)

The Holy Spirit part has confused many people. Just like in a natural marriage, if the marriage is never consummated, it's as if the couple were never married. It is no different in our marriage with Christ. Receiving the Holy Spirit is the consummation of the marriage. It is the seal that binds us to Him and Him to us. In Gen. 4:1, the Bible says that Adam knew Eve his wife; and she conceived. The word knew, in this text, meant sexual intercourse. You see, when our spirit is reconnected with God's spirit or the Holy Spirit, we engage in an intimate relationship with God. Hebrews 8:10, 11 lets us know God's intent for us. It is that all should know God intimately - from the least to the greatest among us. Knowing God is vital because, when he decides to come back, we don't want to hear him say "depart from me, I never knew you". You can follow every tradition, every law, every man made rule, but if you don't have a personal relationship with God and have not been born again, you will not enter the kingdom. He will say I never knew you. (Matt. 7:21-23). Evangelists are responsible for getting new converts to and through the born again process.

Philip, one of the seven deacons in the Jerusalem church, was an evangelist preached and performed miracles in Samaria, converted Simon Magus, and met and baptized an Ethiopian man, a eunuch in Gaza, traditionally marking the start of the Ethiopian Church (Acts 8). Later, he lived in Caesarea Maritima with his four daughters who prophesied, where he was visited by Paul (Acts 21).

We find according to scripture that Jesus was a great evangelist. Throughout the gospels, we find Jesus being followed by multitudes of people. Many have marveled at his awesome gift to gather multitudes of people together. Let's take a look at how he did it.

And it came to pass, that, as the people pressed upon him to hear the word of God, he stood by the lake of Gennesaret. And saw two ships standing by the lake: but the fishermen were gone out of them, and were washing their nets. And he entered into one of the ships, which was Simon's and prayed him that he would thrust out a little from the land.

And he sat down, and taught the people out of the ship. Now when he had left speaking, he said unto Simon, launch out into the deep, and let down your nets for a draught. And Simon answering said unto him, Master, we have toiled all the night and have taken nothing: nevertheless: at thy word I will let down the net. And when they had this done they enclosed a great multitude of fishes: and their net brake. And they beckoned unto their partners, which were in the other ship, that they should come and help them. And they came, and filled both the ships, so that they began to sink. When Simon Peter saw it, he fell down at Jesus' knees, saying, depart from me; for I am a sinful man, O Lord. For he was astonished, and all that were with him, at the draught of the fishes which they had taken: And so was also James, and John, the sons of Zebedee, which were partners with Simon. And Jesus said unto Simon, Fear not; from henceforth thou shalt catch men. And when they had brought their ships to land, they forsook all, and followed him. (Luke 5:1-11).

This particular passage of scripture shows us a strategic way that Jesus evangelized, or gathered people. The first thing we must notice is the fact that he was already being followed by others as verse 1 tells us. <u>Real leaders are always being</u>

followed whether it be intentionally or not. Secondly, Jesus was smart enough to go to their place of interest/passion and showed his knowledge and experience in that area. Jesus understood that being amongst the people gave him access to action. He understood that he needed their attention and what better way than to show his skill and supernatural ability in a way that impressed the people.

Jesus' evangelism was visual. Luke 5:1-11

Jesus capitalized on the opportunity to show a better way. When people are lacking in an area, that is our opportunity to evangelize. But we must show visually that our method, our source, our God, is better than what they already have. Okay, Jesus was God, so how do we exercise this form of evangelism? This is where spiritual gifts come in to play.

Charism is simply the Greek word used in the New Testament for "favor" or "gratuitous gift." Charisms or spiritual gifts are special abilities given to Christians by the Holy Spirit to enable them to be powerful channels of God's love and redeeming presence in the world. Whether extraordinary or ordinary, charisms are to be used in charity or service to build up the church.

Jesus used Spiritual gifts to market himself as worthy of being followed. But he chose wisely who he recruited to become his disciples. With that strategy of recruiting and marketing, we see how Jesus gathered the crowds and chose his inner circle.

In the gospels, we find Jesus in various situations where different spiritual gifts are used. I will give a few examples just so we can see how Jesus used these gifts for the work of the ministry. In Matthew 4, we experience Jesus using his gifts of teaching and healing, which opens the door for his teaching ministry of the Sermon on the Mount. In Matthew 10, Jesus is a pastor using the gift of administration, instructing his disciples. In Matthew 14:27 Jesus discerns the disciples fear and reassures them. In Matthew 16 Jesus prophecies Peter's sermon which opened the door of Christian opportunity to Israel on the day of Pentecost. In Mark 2 we find Jesus evangelizing Matthew. In Mark 7:24 we see Jesus giving the Syrophenician woman a word of wisdom. Jesus gives the rich young ruler a word of knowledge in Mark 10:21. Luke 5 shows us Jesus evangelizing Peter, James, and John through his use of the gift of miracles. Jesus is an apostle according to Luke 10. Jesus shows mercy in John 8. John 11 Jesus raises Lazarus from the dead.

Jesus always used the supernatural as his primary evangelism tool - the power gifts of healing and deliverance with the knowledge gifts of discernment, word of wisdom, and word of knowledge.

In Romans 12 we find Paul urging the saints not to think more highly of themselves, understanding that God has dealt every man the measure of faith. Then he talks about the fact that we are many members, but one body. In verse 6, He talks about the gifts given according to the grace that is given to us. He says if you've been given prophecy, then prophecy. If you've been given ministry, or teaching, or exhortation, or ruling, or showing mercy, etc., then use those gifts accordingly. In verse 9, he sums it all up in one word. He says let <u>love</u> be without dissimulation. He summed up the use of spiritual gifts with <u>love.</u> I would like to submit, according to the scriptures, <u>love</u> is outwardly expressed through spiritual gifts. Now, I'm one who needs to know how to do something. I believe that we have found out how to show God's <u>love,</u> by operating in the gifts that have been given to us by God.

The fivefold ministry gifts are for the body of individuals, equipping them for ministry using the spiritual gifts imparted by the Holy Spirit. Well, you might ask, how are they for the body? Well, in order for God to have a body or kingdom, he must evangelize members or citizens to his kingdom. A Kingdom is flat out, no good without citizens.

Let's say a man is having trouble with his car. He has done everything he knows to do. You come and fix his car. I know if I were that man I would come to you the next time my car breaks down. Now that you have him coming to you, you have the opportunity to teach. You offer to teach him to work on his car himself, which will in turn save him money. Life is the same way. When you see someone struggling in life, use that opportunity to evangelize. The catch is you must have something to offer. People aren't going to listen to someone that is just as broken as they are. You must have had some success in this area in order to show your credibility. Once respect and trust is built, then you have successfully evangelized a recruit and now are ready to begin teaching what you know or what you do. The bottom line is; you can't lead without followers.

. . .

Jesus understood that people are most impressed when you can do something they can't. Most people want to follow those who excel in the area of their passion. For instance, most musicians have someone else who came before them they've learned from and support because he/she excelled in that same area of interest or passion. When I listen to the NBA stars of this day, they always talk of Michael Jordan, Magic Johnson or Larry Bird. They speak of how they have patterned their game after someone they watched as a kid. If you think about it, most people who partner with a certain ministry or organization do so because that ministry or organization has the same passion, interest or method they can relate to. So, if you are trying to evangelize Caucasian people to your ministry then you must study Caucasians and the things that motivate and relate to who they are. The same goes for African Americans, Hispanics, business people, drug dealers, poor people, wealthy people, musicians, teenagers, toddlers, whoever your target audience is - you must study them in order be able to connect with them. Why the church hasn't caught on to this for so long, I don't know - but the world has been great at this. The music industry, game industry, sports industry and many more understand that in order to have success in gathering people, they must know the people (their target audience) and find somewhere to connect with them. Then you must develop programs around that study. Jesus was in no way one dimensional. He understood the basic needs and motivations of people and developed his evangelism according to those things. Think about it, most of the gospels talks about his acts of power - healing the sick, raising the dead, and of course feeding the hungry. But he was smart enough to teach on every occasion that presented itself. <u>Good leaders have an instinct for teaching moments.</u> Then to take it a step further, Jesus had leaders of various cultures and backgrounds. If you want a multicultural ministry, you need to have multicultural leadership. As the top man or woman, you cannot do everything and be everything to all people, so get a variety of leaders under you who can be a connection to those who you cannot reach. Luke 5 is particularly significant because the ones he evangelized were to be later appointed apostles. So this was evangelism of leadership. If you want quality leaders in your ministry, then you cannot just sit and expect them to come to you. Notice, according to the scriptures, the disciples were busy working hard. When evangelizing leaders, you don't want someone who is waiting on things to happen. You want those who know how to make things happen.

<u>Good leaders understand their environment.</u> Jesus understood that he was amongst farmers so he acted and spoke appropriately, according to his environment. When you are working amongst businessmen and women, you must know and understand the culture and language of the business arena and conduct yourself according to your environment. Behold, I send you forth as sheep in the midst of wolves: be ye therefore wise as serpents, and harmless as doves. (Matthew 10:16). When a snake is crawling amongst brown grass, the snake's skin turns brown blending in with the grass. The snakes skin changes again when amongst green grass. But the snake is, no less, still a snake. Jesus knew how to blend in with the people and not be changed by the people. <u>Great leaders can be smart and cunning like a snake, but never compromise who they are in the process.</u> Our greatest evangelism efforts come when we are amongst the people of our community. <u>Everywhere we go is an evangelism opportunity.</u> When we are at the car dealership, the hair salon, or the grocery store, evangelism opportunities exist. Better yet what about our workplace? Let's say you are a mechanic working

at a shop. You are having great success and moving up the food chain very quickly. Someone asks you how you got to be so good. You answer with your testimony of how God showed you that your blessing was in mechanics. You explain how God has promised to bless you with your own shop and that you would help advance the kingdom through mechanics. Needless to say now you have an opportunity to share Christ with someone but also you now have a leadership opportunity. You now can take this person and teach them what you know according to how God has blessed you. Before you know it, your protégé will be at church following you because he wants what you have.

Imagine you are a schoolteacher and you have had great success in teaching - all of your students are doing very well academically. A fellow teacher may ask you what you are doing to achieve such success. Here is another opportunity to share Christ and share what God has taught you. Before you know it, that person is following your God and your principles and practices because of your obedience to God, which brought such success.

And Jesus went about all Galilee, teaching in their synagogues, preaching the gospel of the kingdom, and healing all manner of sickness and disease among the people. And his fame went throughout all Syria: and they brought unto him all sick people that were taken with divers diseases and torments, and those which were possessed with devils, and those which were lunatic, and those that had the palsy; and he healed them. And there followed him great multitudes of people from Galilee, and Decapolis, and from Jerusalem, and from Judaea, and from beyond Jordan. (Matthew 4:23-25).

Jesus begins his ministry teaching in their synagogues, and preaching the gospel of the kingdom, and healing all manner of sickness and all manner of disease. Notice in verse 24, that the people were not necessarily impressed with his teaching and preaching, but they brought to him all sick people with divers diseases and torments, and those possessed with devils, and those which were lunatic, and those that had the palsy; and he healed them. <u>Sinners don't have faith</u>. Jesus' evangelism was visual. Many share their testimony in a way that merely tells others of the benefits that brought them to Christ. This is not evangelism and will end in a typical "good for you" response. Personal testimonies must communicate how the gospel has changed their lives, and be relevant to the listeners if evangelism is going to happen through them. Some people mistake social action or political involvement for evangelism. But many of the problems that we face in our society are usually a symptom of a breach in our vertical relationship with God. Evangelism that stops with meeting felt needs, helping out at the food pantry, or being politically active is surface evangelism. It certainly is needed but lacks any resemblance to the witness of Jesus and his evangelism of power. Peter, James, and John saw all the fish and the multitudes saw the healing. <u>But we cannot evangelize with just great sermons. We cannot evangelize with just good works. We must evangelize with the power of God.</u> We must show the world those things that only God can do. Let me explain a little more in detail about the statement that I made earlier. It's true sinners don't have faith. They can only operate in a measure of faith based on what they've heard. The bible says that faith cometh by hearing, and hearing by the word of God (Rom 10:17). To say that sinners have faith would be to indicate that they possess the Holy Spirit. Faith is a characteristic of the Holy Spirit according to Galatians 5:22. We all know that sinners don't have the Holy Spirit. What is the cardinal rule for sinners? "Seeing is believing." Yes, for most people who are not saved, they judge things from what their eyes tell them. If it looks good to the eye, then it is good according to worldly wisdom. This is why we can't continue to stay broke, busted, and disgusted. This is why we can't continue to live beneath our privilege of love, joy, and peace. If God promised it, we must receive it and display it to the world so that they can see and want what we have. You see exercising faith has nothing to do with sight. 2 Cor 5:7 says we walk by faith, not by sight. Faith functions by hearing not seeing. If you can see it, faith is not involved. Anybody can believe for something that they see. But can you believe for something you can't see? You just heard about it. God spoke to you about a business. You've never taken any kind of business classes or anything, but God said a business. Faith is generated by that word you heard. We must follow our example, Jesus, and take evangelism out of the church building to our communities in every arena and win the world back for the Kingdom.

Another issue I would like to tackle concerning evangelism is the title and how it's used. An evangelist is one who makes new disciples or gathers new recruits into the kingdom. Over the years, I have seen and heard many people refer to themselves as evangelists because they travel from church to church preaching to already made disciples. How do I say this nicely? That is not the function of an evangelist. You did not gather those people in that church. That pastor did. When a man or woman goes to an established church in the kingdom to preach or minister, they are not operating in the function of an evangelist. They can only be operating in one of the other four of the five ascension gifts according to Ephesians 4:11. And since that church is already established, it should have at the least a pastor and teacher and they should be functioning as a prophet or an apostle. This is one of the big issues in the body of Christ. We have so called leaders who don't know who they are and they are trying to do someone else's job. By the way an evangelist is not gender specific either. Just because a person is a female doesn't make them an evangelist. We have many denominations that place titles of evangelists on women just because the title evangelist may sound the most feminine. None of the fivefold ministry gifts are gender specific. And just because a person is of a certain gender does not mean she has been called by God to be an evangelist. I know many women who are powerful teachers, pastors, prophets, and apostles. These women do not have the grace to function as an evangelist.

"Evangelists create converts, while apostles create disciples" (Kim Terrell 2002:22). Their strongest conviction is to see people come into the kingdom, then leaving the discipling to others. They love teaching others how to win people, and never feel like they are actually doing enough. While they are grieved to see believers' lack of urgency regarding the lost, they do have an anointing to impart God's broken heart to the body. Evangelists are absolutely crucial for numeric growth in the local church and the kingdom of God. Imagine if your local church had a group of real evangelists in the church really functioning in their calling and bringing new converts into the Kingdom and mentoring them into the church. How quickly could a church grow with people who are gifted and especially skilled and called in the area of evangelism. Instead of a church growing based on the personality of a leader. The church is actually growing because the people are functioning in their calling. You see the fivefold ministry is not about individuals holding a title but not functioning properly according to the job description of that title. The fivefold ministry represents the five departments of the local church. Every ministry gift and calling functions under one of these five job descriptions. The evangelism department in a local church is where customers of the Kingdom are converted to become employees of the Kingdom. Every business needs a marketing/recruiting department in order to have customers and/or employees. A business without customers and a business without employees simply cannot last. Many churches after they reach a certain level seem to stop making evangelism a priority. But that isn't wise. In this day and age, people don't sit still anymore. People are changing churches like department stores. They go wherever they get the best deal for what they're looking for. Of course, this isn't right and certainly isn't how God designed for people to operate. But it is the reality of many in the body of Christ. Many are consumer Christians. This church has the best music department, I'll go here. The other church has a better youth group for my children, I want to go here. Many make decisions on where they will attend based on these superficial additions to the church. This ought not be. God is intentional about our lives. He doesn't want us wandering around with no direction for our lives and trying to satisfy spiritual needs through natural means. The bible says "Trust in the Lord with all thine heart and lean not to our own understanding, in all thy ways acknowledge him and he will direct our path. (Proverbs 3:5) A relationship with God affords us the benefit of having clear direction for our lives. The steps of a good man are ordered by the Lord: and he delighteth in his way. (Psalms 37:23)

When looking at the recruiting strategy of Jesus we must understand the importance of recruiting and recruiting the right people. Every leader in any capacity will tell you how important it is to recruit the right people. When recruiting, it is important to recruit according to specific skills and needs.

And so *was* also James, and John, the sons of Zebedee, which were partners with Simon. And Jesus said unto Simon, Fear not; from henceforth thou shalt catch men. (Luke 5:10)

In order to gather, who better to recruit than men who gather fish for a living. They can take the principles of gathering fish and use them to gather people. Bait!!!!!!!!!!!!!

Six of the 12 disciples were fisherman, one treasurer, and one tax collector, others unknown. These were professional people with specific skills who provided for specific needs of the ministry.

Recruiting is vital to evangelism in any ministry. Recruiting the right people, with specific skills, to fill specific needs. On the other end Jesus used what is called the marketing concept. The marketing concept is the promotion of business products or services to a targeted audience. Meeting needs and wants is critical to every organization. Effective evangelism will take a team of individuals totally sold out for Christ. Willing to lay their lives down for the Kingdom. Preaching and teaching is not enough. We need signs, wonders and miracles.

And they went forth, and preached everywhere, the Lord working with *them*, and confirming the word with signs following. Amen. (Mark 16:20) KJV

And these signs shall follow them that believe; In my name shall they cast out devils; they shall speak with new tongues; (Mark 16:17) KJV.

Friends if you don't already have an evangelism strategy, I pray that you'll consider these concepts and principles and add them to what you're already doing so that we can be effective in advancing the Kingdom. We don't win the lost at any cost, we win the lost God's way.

6

TEACHING - BRAZEN LAVER (MULTIPLY)

(TRAINING DEPARTMENT)

Teachers are essential in the body of Christ, to give the sheep a good foundation in the word of God. Teachers teach and edify the church, illuminating the scriptures and bringing forth truth that has never before been seen by their listeners.

Jesus recognized how evangelism and teaching work together. You don't have anyone to teach unless the people are evangelized or gathered first. Jesus shows a clear picture of this in Matthew 5:1, 2. Now when Jesus saw the crowds, he went up on a mountainside and sat down. His disciples came to him, and he began to teach them. Jesus taught them from Matthew 5 all the way to chapter 7 verse 28. When Jesus had finished saying these things, the crowds were amazed at his teaching, because he taught as one who had authority, and not as their teachers of the law. Friends, evangelists need teachers and teachers need evangelists. Evangelists can't go and teach. Teachers need evangelists, otherwise they have no one to teach and evangelists need teachers so they can go and know that those fish they've caught will be well taken care of.

Jesus' teaching was very aggressive and controversial, yet practical and progressive. He loved to go against what the popular opinion was. He often used phrases like "Ye have heard that it was said by them of old time" or "It hath been said," He was very much against tradition and religion. Tradition and religion block relationship growth. God's idea was to have a relationship with his people. He wanted a relationship that would grow line upon line and precept upon precept, so that we would grow from faith to faith and glory to glory. "And the Lord said, forasmuch as this people draw near Me with their mouth and honor Me with their lips but remove their hearts and minds far from Me, and their fear and reverence for Me are a commandment of men that is learned by repetition [without any thought as to the meaning]," (Isaiah 29:13 AMP).

Teaching - Brazen Laver (Multiply)

So the Pharisees and scribes asked Jesus, "Why do Your disciples not live their lives according to the tradition of the elders, but [instead] eat their bread with [ceremonially] unwashed hands?" He replied, "Rightly did Isaiah prophesy about you hypocrites (play-actors, pretenders), as it is written [in Scripture], 'These people honor Me with their lips, But their heart is far from Me. 'They worship Me in vain [their worship is meaningless and worthless, a pretense], Teaching the precepts of men as doctrines [giving their traditions equal weight with the Scriptures].' You disregard *and* neglect the commandment of God, and cling [faithfully] to the tradition of men." He was also saying to them, "You are experts at setting aside *and* nullifying the commandment of God in order to keep your [man-made] tradition *and* regulations. For Moses said, 'Honor your father and your mother [with respect and gratitude]'; and, 'He who speaks evil of his father or mother must be put to death'; but you [Pharisees and scribes] say, 'If a man tells his father or mother, "Whatever I have that would help you is Corban, (that is to say, *already* a gift to God),"' then you no longer let him do anything for his father or mother [since helping them would violate his vow of Corban]; so you nullify the [authority of the] word of God [acting as if it did not apply] because of your tradition which you have handed down [through the elders]. And you do many things such as that."

— MARK 7:5-13 AMP

Your relationship with God was never meant to be built through traditions of men. It was meant to be built by revelation. It's through teaching that we learn of God, but through revelation that we see God. Teaching allows us to recognize God when he reveals himself to us, so we respond appropriately. "When Jesus came to the region of Caesarea Philippi, he asked his disciples, "Who do people say the Son of Man is?" They replied, "Some say John the Baptist; others say Elijah; and still others, Jeremiah or one of the prophets." "But what about you?" he asked. "Who do you say I am?" Simon Peter answered, "You are the Christ, the Son of the living God." Jesus replied, "Blessed are you, Simon son of Jonah, for this was not revealed to you by man, but by my Father in heaven. And I tell you that you are Peter, and on this rock I will build my church, and the gates of

Hades will not overcome it. I will give you the keys of the kingdom of heaven; whatever you bind on earth will be bound in heaven, and whatever you loose on earth will beg loosed in heaven." Then he warned his disciples not to tell anyone that he was the Christ" (Matthew 16:20 NIV). This portion of scripture is vital to the spiritual growth of believers. What we must understand is that the church, the kingdom, is not the buildings we worship in. The church, the kingdom, is in us. Jesus tells Peter, by revelation I will build my church. God's plan is to build each individual through revelation, line upon line and precept upon precept so that we grow from faith to faith and glory to glory. "It was he who gave some to be apostles, some to be prophets, some to be evangelists, and some to be pastors and teachers, to prepare God's people for works of service, so that the body of Christ may be **built** up until we all reach unity in the faith and in the knowledge of the Son of God and become mature, attaining to the whole measure of the fullness of Christ" (Ephesians 4:11-13). Once revelation has taken place, the power to bind and loose concerning that revelation is authorized.

Jesus was also practical in his parables, which painted pictures that the people could relate to and understand. He understood the different learning styles. For example, in Matt 13:3-9, Jesus teaches the mysteries of the kingdom of heaven with a story of a sower. This was done on purpose and with a specific intent. Jesus understood <u>who</u> he was talking to. In that day, most of the population was agricultural people (farmers). So this parable was easy to understand either by hearing, or seeing, or actually doing.

Wisdom is the principal thing; therefore get wisdom: and with all thy getting get understanding. (Proverbs 4:7)

Discretion shall preserve thee, understanding shall keep thee: (Proverbs 2:11). <u>Jesus' goal in teaching was understanding</u>. And he called the multitude, and said unto them, Hear and understand: Not that which goeth into the mouth defileth a man; but that which cometh out of the mouth, this defileth a man. (Matt 15:10,11)

Brethren, be not children in understanding: howbeit in malice be ye children, but in understanding be men. (I Cor 14:20). The biggest mistake teachers make is being unclear. The reason why most are unclear is because either they do not have a <u>main idea</u> or they have too many <u>little ideas</u>.

In teaching, Jesus used a combination of 3 things. He taught, demonstrated, and he let them practice. I believe Jesus understood the nature of man. <u>He understood that people remember 10% of what they hear, 50% of what they hear and see, and 90% of what they hear, see, and do.</u>

Why is teaching so important? I've got several reasons, but I'll just share a couple. You see in leadership there is always a vision in mind. A common goal that all are working together to achieve. With that said, the first reason would be to communicate the vision. In order for the vision to be understood and brought to pass, the people must understand the goals of the vision. Habakkuk 2:2 "Write the vision, and make it plain on tables, that he may run that readeth it". In teaching we must take into account that there are different ways people learn, different levels of education, and many other factors that could hinder understanding. Now first of all, God isn't asking you to do something he hasn't done -that's another leadership lesson. Jesus wrote his vision down. We read it every day. Or for some of us it sits on our living room table as decoration. If it was important for him to write out the vision, I would think that would be something we might consider doing. Even when I think of the significance of the part that the Bible plays in our daily lives. I couldn't imagine trying to do the will of the lord without the Bible. There have been numerous times where I just didn't understand things. The bible has been that one thing that has been able to open my understanding.

<u>Teaching is our means of communicating the vision.</u> People need to know who is doing what, what they are to do, why they are to do it, when they are to do it, where they are to do it, and how they are to do it. Also, the Bible tells us according to Hosea 4:6, My people are destroyed for a lack of knowledge. I noticed in my history studies that advancement in knowledge was instrumental in the survival of civilizations. I have a game called civilizations. In this game we are to build our empire or civilization against other great leaders such as Ghandi, Shaka Zulu, Alexander the Great, Julius Caesar, Cleopatra, and many others. The goal is to build your empire so it will be able to withstand invasion, make a profit off of the culture, and expand if needed for the comfort of your people. What I noticed in playing this game was you must use science and study in order to advance in technology. It is really no fun when your enemy comes against you with airplanes and ships and all you have are foot soldiers with axes.

As you can imagine, the foot soldiers are no match for the airplanes and ships. So I began to notice a race in technology. Technology gives you the advantage over your enemy. Technology now becomes an asset you can use to profit. In this game, I found myself proposing my knowledge in exchange for currency. Then, with the currency, I was able to pay for more knowledge in order to keep me on top. You see, when Jesus came to the earth, he had a vision in mind. He came to reestablish his kingdom on the earth and we as his disciples or fellow citizens of the Kingdom of Heaven must continue to study to show ourselves approved workmen that need not be ashamed, rightly dividing the word of truth. We need God's wisdom and knowledge and understanding so that we can continue in the fight proclaiming the gospel in all the world. Another reason teaching is so important is, <u>without knowledge we are bound to what we currently know.</u> And if what we currently know is not enough then we are stuck with what we know. Ephesians 2:12 says "That at that time ye were without Christ, being aliens from the commonwealth of Israel, and strangers from the covenants of promise, having no hope, and without God in the world". This scripture really identifies some Christians right now. Many of us are living beneath our privilege because they don't know who they are, what they are entitled to, why they are who they are, and the responsibilities and benefits of being who they are. Many people are sick because they don't know that God can heal their bodies. Many people are broke, busted, and disgusted because they don't know that God has promised to give us the power to get wealth. Many people are depressed because they don't know about the joy of the Lord.

Many of you may have seen the movie, The Hair Show. I believe this movie gave us the perfect example of what happens to many Christians. The movie portrays two young ladies in a lawyer's office for the reading of their grandmother's will. The lawyer begins to explain that the grandmother had left one sister $75,000 and she left the other sister a Bible. Of course, the sister who was left the Bible went into a rage and stormed out without the bible. Later in the movie, the sisters, who never really got along are reunited again. They argue one last time and the paid sister gives her sister the Bible she left. Finally, with tears streaming down her face she decides to open the bible to find an envelope in the bible. The envelope had a letter and a check in it for $75,000. So what am I getting at? The point is that many of us are broke, busted, and disgusted. Life is just in chaos because we won't take time to find out what the bible has to say about our situation. In this case everything she needed was in that Bible the whole time. It is lack of knowledge that many times keeps us in bondage. Friends every business has a training department. No new employee comes into any business without orientation and training. You can't hold someone accountable to something you've never taught or told them. Our expectations can only rise to the level of training we've provided. Every church, ministry and fellowship must have a group of teachers ready and willing to train God's new employees.

7

PASTOR - TABLE OF SHEWBREAD (REPLENISH THE EARTH)

(SUPERVISORS)

Many theologians relate a pastor to a shepherd. The pastor is the heart of the church. He is a shepherd who deeply cares for his sheep, ready to lie down everything for them. He wants them to be fed, to grow, to be equipped, to develop their giftings, and step into the calling of God for their lives. In the local church, they are the bridge between the different offices and functions, listening to all sides and restoring calm and order where necessary. Jesus, the chief Shepherd, taught a lot about shepherding sheep, He was the great example of what a pastor should look like. The pastor's greatest concern is always the well-being of his sheep and his body, not only bringing training, but correction and protection where necessary.

In my study of a shepherd, he is always leading sheep somewhere. In Ps.23 4 of 6 passages suggest leadership. He leadeth me beside still waters. If you know anything about sheep, sheep will not drink from troubled water. Sheep are very fearful creatures. I know a lot of fearful saints. <u>A good shepherd/leader chooses carefully and strategically where he will stop to drink</u>. The duty of shepherds was to keep their flock intact and protect it from wolves and other predators. The shepherd was also to supervise the migration of the flock and ensure they made it to market areas in time for shearing.

He leadeth me in the path of righteousness for his name sake. Again the shepherd/pastor/leader is taking his sheep somewhere. They are not staying in the same place. <u>According to this scripture, we find that the shepherd would never lead his sheep somewhere that would challenge the integrity of his name</u>.

"Yea, though I walk through the valley of the shadow of death, I will fear no evil; for thou art with me; thy rod and thy staff they comfort me".

Most people if they believe in your vision and trust and respect you, will go through the valley of the shadow of death with you. But I can imagine people leaving and not wanting to go if they fear you can't or won't protect them. The very fact that they can trust that you will be there for them will comfort them while on the journey. Establishing trust and respect is often an ongoing process. But Jesus did it through signs and wonders. He mastered the art of meeting needs and when confronted he was strong and courageous in standing up against the Pharisees and Sadducees. These things helped the disciples as they followed him from place to place.

Pastors need teachers because the sheep need to know what to do and how to do when they get to their destination. Jesus was the perfect pastor providing a platform for the disciples to practice what they had been taught. <u>A good leader always provides everything that is needed to successfully accomplish any task.</u> Watch what Matthew 10:5-10 says: Go not into the way of the Gentiles, and into any city of the Samaritans enter ye not: But go rather to the lost sheep of the house of Israel. And as ye go, preach, saying, The kingdom of heaven is at hand. Heal the sick, cleanse the lepers, raise the dead, cast out devils: freely ye have received, freely give. Provide neither gold, nor silver, nor brass in your purses, nor scrip for your journey, neither two coats, neither shoes, nor yet staves: for the workman is worthy of his meat.

Jesus gave specific instructions, where to go, where not to go, what to do, how to do it, what to take for the journey. I like that he provided for all of their needs. They were to take nothing, for it is the leader's job to provide for the resources and the delegate authority to get the job done. A good pastor knows his people. The bible says to know them that dwell among you. This is vital in leading people. There is nothing worse than being led to the wrong place. Many people are being led to the wrong place because our pastors don't know who their sheep are. There is nothing worse than having an evangelist doing a prophet's job. A prophet's job is to declare truth, not compel men. When you don't know your people, you run the risk of misplacing them in ministry. You want your people functioning in the area that God ordained them to function so the kingdom may be advanced properly and quickly. This makes your job easier when your people are placed properly. Placement in ministry should be according to gifting and calling. I know that it's hard at times to stick to this principle, especially when volunteers are scarce. But the reward will be great and the production level will be great. "A man's gift makes room for him, and brings him before great men" (Proverbs 18:16). When a person is operating in their gift, they will operate with such an excellence that you will be glad you made that decision. That's why Jesus told James and John that he would make them fishers of men. Asking a man to work out of his area of gifting is like asking to a fish to swim on dry land. Fish must be in water in order to do what they do best. The same goes for a gifted man.

In Acts 20:28, we find the biblical exhortation: "Take heed, therefore, unto yourselves, and to all the flock over which the Holy Ghost hath made you overseers, to feed the church of God, which he hath purchased with his own blood." No one can take heed of others until he has first taken heed unto himself. A man can lead another in spiritual things only in proportion to his own understanding and experience.

I Thess. 5:12, 13 reveals the importance of understanding the relationship between pastor and people in the words:" ... know them which labor among you and are over you in the Lord, and admonish you, and to esteem them very highly in love for their works sake..." Good pastors are vital to the body of Christ in these last days. I'm not just speaking of senior pastors - I'm speaking especially of intermediate pastors. Those leaders that are close to the sheep, leading them in different activities of the church. These pastors are vital for accountability and assimilation. Many times we lose sheep without even noticing until they've been gone so long that it's too late.

Again, know them which labor among you. We find in the gospels that Jesus was excellent at this. Jesus understood the culture of the age. He spoke in agricultural terms because he was speaking to agricultural people. When the Pharisees and Sadducees would come to interrogate him, he knew their traditions and was educated in their doctrines. He was able to defend and prove all that he did not just by word of mouth but also through the word which the haters thought they knew.

A person becomes a leader long before he occupies a position or a place of influence. A man is a leader by virtue of his performance rather than by virtue of his position. But when he occupies a position of leadership, his leadership ability should grow and increase. Leadership is both ability and activity. A pastor must know how to work with people, work through people, minister to people, and lead people.

I love this about Jesus' ministry, because this proves John Maxwell's book about leading from the different levels. Jesus led from the bottom to the middle until he eventually made it to the top where he is seated at the right hand of the father. We read in the gospels how Jesus is leading at an early age in the synagogues with the scribes and leaders of the day. He was working his gift early, thus making it easy for him once he came of age. Then as he began his ministry he still wasn't on top. At this point he would have been considered in the middle. Having to minister to all levels of life, he gained influence and a following amongst the poor and needy by meeting their needs, while also ministering to the leaders of the day as they heard of his fame and tried to interrogate and discredit him. Now, he is leading through the Holy Spirit sent from above as Jesus is seated in heavenly places at the right hand of the father.

Pastors don't start churches; they are assigned sheep to watch over. There is no biblical evidence of any pastor starting and building a local church.

The words bishop, elder, overseer, deacon, and pastor are all used interchangeably. They are managers and supervisors of the sheep as they do the work of the ministry.

Since an overseer manages God's household, he must be blameless—not overbearing, not quick-tempered, not given to drunkenness, not violent, not pursuing dishonest gain. (Titus 1:7 NIV)

An elder is a manager of God's household, so he must live a blameless life. He must not be arrogant or quick-tempered; he must not be a heavy drinker, violent, or dishonest with money. (Titus 1:7 NLT)

For a bishop must be blameless, as the steward of God; not self-willed, not soon angry, not given to wine, no striker, not given to filthy lucre; (Titus 1:7 KJV)

The following scriptures shows there to be more than one bishop in a local church

Philippians 1:1

Paul and Timotheus, the servants of Jesus Christ, to all the saints in Christ Jesus which are at Philippi, with the bishops and deacons: (KJV)

Paul and Timothy, servants of Christ Jesus, To all God's holy people in Christ Jesus at Philippi, together with the overseers and deacons: (NIV)

This letter is from Paul and Timothy, slaves of Christ Jesus. I am writing to all of God's holy people in Philippi who belong to Christ Jesus, including the elders and deacons. (NLV)

From: Paul and Timothy, servants of the Messiah Jesus. To: All the holy ones in Philippi, along with their overseers and ministers, who are in union with the Messiah Jesus. (ISV)

Wow, Philippians here is telling us the proper placement for bishops. A bishop is a local church leadership position with supervisory duties within the local church. But many have made it to be something other than how the early church had placed it. Now the office of the bishop is being used as some glamorous position of elite people that operate with a superstar mentality.

When you promote and glamorize man appointed offices (bishop, elder, deacon, and overseer) over divine Godly callings (apostles, prophets, evangelists, pastors and teachers), you open the door to a political, networking Jezebel spirit that comes to take control based on selfish interests.

Friends, our destiny is not to be apostles, prophets, evangelists, pastors and teachers, nor bishop, deacon, overseer or elder. Our destiny is to be conformed to image of his son according to Romans 8:29. Operating as a fivefold ministry gift is the function in which we, by individual assignment display the image of God to others. Our lives should be as a type and shadow of Christ in principle, method, and assignment.

The government system many in the body of Christ are using now is basically a prison system form of government, copied from the Roman Catholic Church. The Senior Pastor is the warden. There are a few elders, who represent the guards. And the rest of the people are the inmates. God never intended it to be this way. A bishop led church will only manage and supervise God's Kingdom. A fivefold ministry led church will build and advance God's Kingdom using all the saints. Bishops, elders, deacons, and overseers were appointed by apostles to supervise or manage the saints doing work of the ministry.

Every believer should be in training and rotation for the work of the ministry. We need to find ways to get more people involved in advancing the Kingdom. If a person is a supervisor on their job, they might serve well as a pastor supervising others doing the work of the ministry. I believe every church should be governed by an Apostolic team consisting of an Apostle and Prophet as the foundational leaders, with fivefold ministry departments consisting of groups of fivefold ministry gifts operating according to the job description of the gift.

8

PROPHECY - GOLDEN CANDLESTICKS (SUBDUE)

(ADVISORS)

What is prophecy? Prophecy is the speaking forth of the mind and counsel of God. The purpose of prophecy is edification, exhortation, and comfort of the believers.

I Corinthians 14:3 says, "He that prophesieth speaketh unto men edification, and exhortation, and comfort." The amplified says it like this, "But [on the other hand], the one who prophesies [who interprets the divine will and purpose in inspired preaching and teaching] speaks to men for their upbuilding and constructive spiritual progress and encouragement and consolation" (I Corinthians 14:3). The purpose and priority of prophecy is understanding. I would that ye all spake with tongues, but rather that ye prophesied: for greater is he that prophesieth than he that speaketh with tongues, except he interpret, that the church may receive edifying. (I Cor 14:5)

There are times when a "spirit of prophecy" rests on a meeting when anyone can prophesy. Paul laid hands on twelve disciples at Ephesus to receive the Holy Ghost, they "spake with tongues, and prophesied" (Acts 19:5). If I were to say to someone that they are fearfully and wonderfully made, I just prophesied to them. I spoke the word of God to them.

A higher level of prophecy, is the Gift of Prophecy. This level requires more faith and a greater anointing. This gift is manifested through a more spiritually mature person who is considered a "specialist" in the prophetic gift.

The Prophet is the highest level, which is a specially called office or ministry being equipped with the necessary gifts and fellow ministers recognizing the special call of God upon the prophet's life. In this portion, I want to focus on the Gift of Prophecy and the Office of the Prophet.

In biblical times, prophets foretold the future, condemned unrighteous acts, gave encouragement, offered instruction and direction concerning specific situations, interpreted dreams and recommended courses of action for rulers and priests. You see, in the context of the prophet being a part of the fivefold ministry team, we must consider that the prophet would be confirming the call on a person's life, giving encouragement, offering instruction and direction as it relates to destiny. This reminds me of Moses at the burning bush in Exodus 3 when he was being called and sent to Egypt to be God's channel of deliverance for the children of Israel. "Go, assemble the elders of Israel and say to them, 'The Lord, the God of your fathers—the God of Abraham, Isaac and Jacob—appeared to me and said: I have watched over you and have seen what has been done to you in Egypt. And I have promised to bring you up out of your misery in Egypt into the land of the Canaanites, Hittites, Amorites, Perizzites, Hivites and Jebusites—a land flowing with milk and honey.'

"The elders of Israel will listen to you. Then you and the elders are to go to the king of Egypt and say to him, 'The Lord, the God of the Hebrews, has met with us. Let us take a three-day journey into the desert to offer sacrifices to the Lord our God.' But I know that the king of Egypt will not let you go unless a mighty hand compels him. So I will stretch out my hand and strike the Egyptians with all the wonders that I will perform among them. After that, he will let you go.

"And I will make the Egyptians favorably disposed toward this people, so that when you leave you will not go empty-handed. Every woman is to ask her neighbor and any woman living in her house for articles of silver and gold and for clothing, which you will put on your sons and daughters. And so you will plunder the Egyptians" (Exodus 3:16:22).

In these passages we notice the foretelling of the future, offering of instructions and directions and encouragement. God shares with Moses his intent for delivering the Children of Israel, what he must do in this process and what to do when they are released.

We see a similar prophetic word to Noah in Genesis 6. So God said to Noah, "I am going to put an end to all people, for the earth is filled with violence because of them. I am surely going to destroy both them and the earth. So make yourself an ark of cypress wood; make rooms in it and coat it with pitch inside and out. This is how you are to build it: The ark is to be 450 feet long, 75 feet wide and 45 feet high. Make a roof for it and finish the ark to within 18 inches of the top. Put a door in the side of the ark and make lower, middle and upper decks. I am going to bring floodwaters on the earth to destroy all life under the heavens, every creature that has the breath of life in it. Everything on earth will perish. But I will establish my covenant with you, and you will enter the ark—you and your sons and your wife and your sons' wives with you. You are to bring into the ark two of all living creatures, male and female, to keep them alive with you. Two of every kind of bird, of every kind of animal and of every kind of creature that moves along the ground will come to you to be kept alive. You are to take every kind of food that is to be eaten and store it away as food for you and for them."

Noah did everything just as God commanded him.

Jesus also prophesies to Simon Peter after the revelation of who he was in Matthew 16. He not only confirmed who Peter was, but spoke of Peter opening the door of Christian opportunity to Israel on the day of Pentecost and to Gentiles in the house of Cornelius.

And he said unto them, I beheld Satan as lightning fall from heaven. Behold, I give unto you power to tread on serpents and scorpions, and over all the power of the enemy: and nothing shall by any means hurt you. (Luke 10:18)

Not only did he confirm what the seventy had just experienced, but he encourages them to continue with a promise of protection.

Again, we are discussing the role of the prophet within the fivefold ministry team. The prophet edifies, exhorts, and comforts the believers. He also assists in directing the believer toward destiny

Personal prophecy will always be partial, progressive, and conditional.

Prophecy is only a small look into the will of God for our lives. "For we know in part, and we prophesy in part" (1 Cor. 13:9). We should never prophesy as if we have the full picture. Only God knows and has the full picture. God always gives just enough to help us do what he wants us to do at that particular place and time. Prophecy is also progressive. Each additional prophecy should build upon the previous prophecy and unfold over the years. Abraham was a prime example of progressive prophecy. In the beginning, God gave Abraham instructions to leave his country into a land that he would show him. And throughout the rest of Abraham's life, God gave him further instructions as needed.

Prophecy also at times deals with the present with futuristic content. For example, Joseph when interpreting Pharaoh's dream, gives specific instructions as to what to do in preparation for what was coming. Joseph, while interpreting Pharaoh's dream, told Pharaoh to appoint commissioners to take a fifth of the harvest of Egypt during the seven years of abundance. This food was to be held in reserve for the country to be used during the seven years of famine. (Genesis 41)

"A man or woman who represents the interests of God to the people. Having stood in the council of God, the prophet releases a clarion call to the people of what is in God's heart at the moment." (Goll 2001:294)

Prophets reveal the mind of God to His people, giving guidance to individuals and the body, giving revelation, as well as often interpretation, application and timing.

In Jeremiah 1:10, God gives the general functions of the prophet.

1. to pluck (root) up — "weeds," both in the

lives of individual believers, as well as "weeds" growing in the Church, which is false teaching and brethren.
2. to break down — resistances and rebellion to God's Word, Will, and Way by believers.
3. to destroy — vain philosophies and imaginations raised up against the knowledge of God and Satan's works.
4. to overthrow — the kingdoms of men; and strongholds of the devil.
5. to build — the Church spiritually upon the foundation of the Life of Christ.
6. to plant — Christ as the Seed of God in the Church and in the individual lives of believers; and, along with Apostles — plant Churches.

In my opinion the best prophetic words are those that have a combination of word of knowledge, word of wisdom, and prophecy altogether. Let's look at a couple in the bible.

Now the earth was corrupt in God's sight and was full of violence. God saw how corrupt the earth had become, for all the people on earth had corrupted their ways. So God said to Noah, "I am going to put an end to all people, for the earth is filled with violence because of them. I am surely going to destroy both them and the earth. So make yourself an ark of cypress wood; make rooms in it and coat it with pitch inside and out. This is how you are to build it: The ark is to be three hundred cubits long, fifty cubits wide and thirty cubits high. Make a roof for it, leaving below the roof an opening one cubit high all around. Put a door in the side of the ark and make lower, middle and upper decks. I am going to bring

floodwaters on the earth to destroy all life under the heavens, every creature that has the breath of life in it. Everything on earth will perish. But I will establish my covenant with you, and you will enter the ark—you and your sons and your wife and your sons' wives with you. You are to bring into the ark two of all living creatures, male and female, to keep them alive with you. Two of every kind of bird, of every kind of animal and of every kind of creature that moves along the ground will come to you to be kept alive. You are to take every kind of food that is to be eaten and store it away as food for you and for them." Noah did everything just as God commanded him. (Genesis 6:11-22)

SEE THE COMBINATION

The earth was corrupt and full of violence – **Word of knowledge**

Detailed instructions for the Ark – **Word of Wisdom**

It's going to flood on earth and destroy all life – **Prophecy**

Friends, with only the word of knowledge the person only gets confirmation of their present or past situation. Well I'm sure the person knew that already, but they are probably impressed that you knew it. But it doesn't help them to do anything about their situation. You see, adding the word of wisdom to it, now the person has something to work with. The word of wisdom says hey this is what you need to do. And then the prophecy confirms what eventually will happen. Without the word of wisdom Noah and his family die in the flood with everyone else.

The story of Joseph gives us another picture of this combination. You can find it in Genesis 41:17-40

Joseph interprets the dream – **Word of Knowledge**

Instructions to collect the food and store – **Word of wisdom**

There will be a famine – **Prophecy**

Again without the word of wisdom regardless of the interpretation of the dream, the people would have still died in the famine because of the lack of wisdom to collect and store the food for the time of famine. We can no longer accept these fluffy prophetic words with no real connection to where I am, where I'm going, and how I'm gonna get there. We need prophetic excellence in this hour. God is raising up prophets with answers not just diagnosis. Prophetic ministry is an advisory function in the church.

We need prophets to advise the evangelism department, music department, community activism department, security, administrative department, etc. We need prophets who can bring solutions to problems.

9

APOSTLE - ALTAR OF INCENSE (HAVE DOMINION)
(ADMINISTRATORS)

To be an apostle is to be one who sends. But to send, you must also be sent. Jesus reminded us consistently that he was sent for the advancement of the Kingdom. Jesus, after he had evangelized, taught, pastored, and prophesied, is in the final phase of his mission (now after his resurrection), which is to send forth his chosen apostles. Their job would be the same, which was to evangelize, teach, pastor, prophesy, and send (apostle).

And, being assembled together with them, commanded them that they should not depart from Jerusalem, but wait for the promise of the Father, which, saith he, ye have heard of me. (Acts 1:4)

But ye shall receive power, after that the Holy Ghost is come upon you: and ye shall be witnesses unto me both in Jerusalem, and in all Judaea, and in Samaria, and unto the uttermost part of the earth. And when he had spoken these things, while they beheld, he was taken up; and a cloud received him out of their sight.

This is a classic example of true apostleship. The apostle's main concern is always that the mission continues when he/she is gone. The true heart of an apostle is succession. Apostles understand that the mission is bigger than they are.

As they ministered to the Lord, and fasted, the Holy Ghost said, Separate me Barnabas and Saul for the work whereunto I have called them. (Acts 13:2)

I find it very interesting that Paul, after his conflict with Barnabas over Mark, didn't just go out on his own - ut chose to take Silas with him. My opinion of this was he wanted to stay with the structure Jesus had used during his time on the earth. Jesus always according to scripture sent them forth two by two. (Acts 15:39, 40)

Jim Goll (2001:290) defines an apostle as, "one called and sent by Christ to have the spiritual authority, character, gifts and abilities to reach and establish people in Kingdom truth and order, especially through founding and overseeing local churches." An apostle has, "a burden to build something that didn't exist before" (Kim Terrell 2002:17). Apostles lay the foundation of new local churches and see to it that they come into full maturity. That is the church that person will be the apostle to – which means he/she will not have any authority as an apostle in other churches, which is what many today claim. Paul himself wrote to the Corinthians, Even though I may not be an apostle to others, surely I am to you! For you are the seal of my apostleship in the Lord (1 Corinthians 9:2).

Apostles have a burden to grow their church in solid biblical teaching, an example of which we can see in Acts 11, when Paul and Barnabas spent two years at Antioch, teaching and equipping them. Apostles have the desire to train and raise up kingdom leaders who will come into full maturity in the church, to impact the community they serve, and then move on to plant another church. Making themselves "redundant" is their greatest reward, as they father their spiritual children into adulthood.

Apostles have the unique ability to care about all the things that the other four care about - but with balance. They (apostles) recognize that all five gifts are vital to the proper growth and maturity of the body of Christ. That's one reason why apostles are represented on the hand as the thumb, because they can relate to and touch all the other four fingers. Apostles always have unity and maturity at the forefront of their mind.

Apostles have the colonization mindset and understand we can only send the mature because they will be strong and courageous. They also understand the need for unity because unity is important to expanding the kingdom in a way that represents God's original plan.

Let's look at some characteristics of true apostles according to scriptures. In his book the last Apostles on earth, Roger Sapp lists five characteristics of true apostles.

1. Signs, wonders, and miracles. "Truly the signs of an apostle were wrought among you in all patience, in signs, and wonders, and mighty deeds" (II Corinthians 12:12 KJV). The ministry of an apostle will

always include healing and deliverance, casting out of demons, and operating in the supernatural.

2. Revelation of the Calling to Independent Witnesses. "In the church at Antioch there were prophets and teachers: Barnabas, Simeon called Niger, Lucius of Cyrene, Manaen (who had been brought up with Herod the tetrarch) and Saul. While they were worshiping the Lord and fasting, the Holy Spirit said, "Set apart for me Barnabas and Saul for the work to which I have called them." So after they had fasted and prayed, they placed their hands on them and sent them off" (Acts 13:1-3 NIV). God will always confirm his calling on your life through credible individuals who have been witness to your character, ministry, and life.

3. Ministers are given to Apostles. "He was accompanied by Sopater son of Pyrrhus from Berea, Aristarchus and Secundus from Thessalonica, Gaius from Derbe, Timothy also, and Tychicus and Trophimus from the province of Asia" (Acts 20:4 NIV). Apostles are big

advocates for team ministry. Therefore, God surrounds them with ministers to work together in harmony under their authority.

4. Fully functional churches. "Even though I may not be an apostle to others, surely I am to you! For you are the seal of my apostleship in the Lord" (I Corinthians 9:2 NIV). Apostles have repeated success in church planting.

5. Serious resistance from evil prince angels. "And lest I should be exalted above measure through the abundance of the revelations, there was given to me a thorn in the flesh, the messenger of Satan to buffet me, lest I should be exalted above measure" (II Corinthians 12:7 KJV). Apostolic ministry is always met with great opposition. Many think that because a ministry is accepted and received by the masses, that the ministry is blessed by God. This is not true. If there is no opposition, then there's no proof of your power.

Apostles are essential for this fivefold ministry team working together in harmony and unity.

They bring balance and a calculated approach to giving the body what it needs when it needs it. Apostles put out the fires of disagreement among the other gifts and use each gift when needed to create a harmonious flow of the Holy Spirit.

10

THE FIVEFOLD MINISTRY & THE TABERNACLE
A LOCAL CHURCH PATTERN

As previously stated, God's original intent for his people was to be a kingdom that he would rule over. It was never God's intent for there to be this many different organizations, fellowships, denominations, etc. As I am very aware that God works differently with individuality concerning spiritual gifts, I don't believe that I Corinthians 12 is applicable to the structure and government of the local church.

Paul was very clear in Ephesians 2:19, 20 where he explains the foundational leadership structure of the church. Earlier, I explained the comparison of the Apostle, Prophet, and Holy Spirit with the Prophet, Priest, and King functions. The principle of two with the Holy Spirit as the third and chief cornerstone has just flat out been ignored. It's not that people don't know - the bible has plenty of examples from the Old Testament to the New Testament that prove that this is the pattern that God has ordained. I will be blunt and honest, there are many who know about this but refuse because of selfishness and greed. Many are using the ministry to build up their stocks as opposed to building the kingdom. But the thing that's comforting is, God knew all of this would happen. Again, I am speaking from the perspective of God's original intent. I realize that many have been taught differently over the years and already have ministries that aren't structured in this fashion. My response to those who find themselves in this situation is to seek God as to how to fix it.

It's imperative that all five of the gifts be in operation. The sheep need them. I've been all over the world as a military man and been a part of a great ministry, but the majority of the ministries that I've had the privilege of attending did not have all five gifts operating together in harmony. There are some, but I believe it was God's intent for all local churches to look like his son Jesus'.

So what does the governmental structure of the local church look like? It looks like and is structured like the Tabernacle of Moses. The Tabernacle was set up with two sets of leaders that I call the foundational and ministry leaders. The foundational leadership was made up of God as King, Moses as the Prophet, and Aaron as the Priest. Eventually according to Deuteronomy 17, God allows the King position to be filled by a human being of his choosing. The first King that Israel gets is Saul.

Let's talk about the King function. The most notable function we have of God as King was that he established and administrated policy and law. We know this by the three laws the Children of Israel lived by - the Moral, Ceremonial, and Civil laws. The moral law was a combination of justice and mercy. All the requirements of God's moral law hang on two principles. "Thou shalt love the Lord thy God with all thine heart, and with all thy soul, and with all thy might" (Deut 6:5). The second one is ""Thou shalt love thy neighbor as thyself"(Leviticus 19:18). The Moral Law speaks of righteousness, but has no power to redeem those that break it.

The Ceremonial Law governed the tabernacle, the sacrificial offerings, and the priestly ministry. Every ordinance of the Ceremonial Law pointed to

Christ and his work of saving man from sin. Every function the priests performed symbolized Christ's ministry in the Heavenly Sanctuary. The Moral Law defines the conduct of the righteous, the Ceremonial Law had to do with the plan of salvation and God's work of grace for the repentant, believing sinner. It was through the Ceremonial Law that the righteousness of God was able to be "witnessed by the law and the prophets.

Every country, kingdom, or state has civil regulations and the God-given authority for enforcing law and order. So God gave Israel, his Kingdom, laws governing the administration of justice. These laws were not tribal, but for the whole nation. Israel was subject to these laws in the same way in which we are subject to the laws of the land in which we live.

So the King's function was that of the administrator. An administrator is one who administers affairs; one who directs, manages, executes, or dispenses, whether in civil, judicial, political, or ecclesiastical affairs. God as King also performed many signs and wonders in the eyes of his people. This is very much like the function of the Apostles in the New Testament. The Apostles laid foundation of the church (Ephesians 2:20; Matthew 16:18), gave God's revelation to men (Ephesians 3:5) and demonstrated power through signs and wonders (II Corinthians 12:12).

So with that information, we must go back to the point of God as King, Moses as the Prophet, and Aaron as the Priest. During Jesus' ministry on the earth he functioned in all three capacities. But now we have the three functions in the church age with the Apostles operating in the King capacity, Prophets remain in the same capacity, and the Holy Spirit functioning in the capacity of the Priest (Ephesians 2:20). The Apostle is not the King - he/she operates in the function and position of the King, in the same manner that Saul, David, and Solomon did. This pattern of Apostle, Prophet, and Holy Spirit is God's intent for foundational leadership for the local church. It would look something like this:

Holy Spirit

Apostle   Prophet

A person standing alone can be attacked and defeated, but two can stand back-to-back and conquer. Three are even better, for a triple-braided cord is not easily broken (Ecclesiastes 4:12 NLT). It is with this revelation that I believe that those who are the founders of a local church actually are operating in the function of an apostle. I also believe that those who are appointed to lead a flock are operating in the function of the pastor. With this belief, the practice of succession is key for the vision to come to pass and continue as God originally designed it. Now, I understand how many believe in pastoring until they die. In Moses' case, that was very clear. Also, David wasn't able to take over as King until Saul had been killed. But the difference in these two examples is Moses clearly taught Joshua the vision and because of that, proper succession took place. Also the bible says Joshua did all that the Lord told Moses to do. You see, when a founding pastor or apostle passes away, lack of continuity should not be an issue because, in life, he or she should have been grooming someone to take his or her place and continue on with the founding vision. If you will notice in Joshua chapter 18, Joshua kept with the structural government that Moses and Aaron operated in with Eleazar the son of Aaron, the priest, operating in the function of the priest.

The next level of leadership that we see in the Tabernacle of Moses was the Levitical Priesthood, which is represented by the fivefold ministry. In Numbers 3, God tells Moses to ordain Aaron's sons Eleazar and Ithamar as priests to minister with their father Aaron in the Tent of Meeting (Tabernacle) as priests. Eleazar and Ithamar represent the ministry gifts of the apostle and prophet as read in Ephesians 4:11. Then God tells Moses to bring the Tribe of Levi to Aaron the priest. They are to perform duties for him and the whole community at the Tent of Meeting (Tabernacle) by doing the work of the tabernacle (Numbers 3:5-10). Doesn't work of the tabernacle sound familiar? It sounds familiar to the expression work of the ministry in Ephesians 4. "And His gifts were [varied; He Himself appointed and gave men to us] some to be apostles (special messengers), some prophets (inspired preachers and expounders), some evangelists (preachers of the Gospel, traveling missionaries), some pastors (shepherds of His flock) and teachers. His intention was the perfecting and the full equipping of the saints (His consecrated people), [that they should do] the work of ministering toward building up Christ's body (the church), [That it might develop] until we all attain oneness in the faith and in the comprehension of the [full and accurate] knowledge of the Son of God, that [we might arrive] at really mature manhood (the completeness of personality which is nothing less than the standard height of Christ's own perfection), the measure of the stature of the fullness of the Christ and the completeness found in Him (Ephesians 4:11-13AMP).

So now that Aaron has the help of the Levites, we find that Levi had three sons Gershon, Kohath, and Merari.

"The Gershonite clans were to camp on the west, behind the tabernacle. The leader of the families of the Gershonites was Eliasaph son of Lael. At the Tent of Meeting the Gershonites were responsible for the care of the tabernacle and tent, its coverings, the curtain at the entrance to the Tent of Meeting, the curtains of the courtyard, the curtain at the entrance to the courtyard surrounding the tabernacle and altar, and the ropes—and everything related to their use" (Numbers 3:23-26 NIV).

"The Kohathites were responsible for the care of the sanctuary. The Kohathite clans were to camp on the south side of the tabernacle. The leader of the families of the Kohathite clans was Elizaphan son of Uzziel. They were responsible for the care of the ark, the table, the lampstand, the altars, the articles of the sanctuary used in ministering, the curtain, and everything related to their use. The chief leader of the Levites was Eleazar son of Aaron, the priest. He was appointed over those who were responsible for the care of the sanctuary" (Numbers 3:28-32 NIV).

"The leader of the families of the Merarite clans was Zuriel son of Abihail; they were to camp on the north side of the tabernacle. The Merarites were appointed to take care of the frames of the tabernacle, its crossbars, posts, bases, all its equipment, and everything related to their use, as well as the posts of the surrounding courtyard with their bases, tent pegs and ropes" (Numbers 3:35-37 NIV).

"Moses and Aaron and his sons were to camp to the east of the tabernacle, toward the sunrise, in front of the Tent of Meeting. They were responsible for the care of the sanctuary on behalf of the Israelites. Anyone else who approached the sanctuary was to be put to death" (Numbers 3:38 NIV).

So now we have five sets of families responsible for doing the work of the tabernacle. Eleazar, and

Ithamar, the sons of Aaron and Gershon, Kohath, and Merari, sons of Levi. These represent the fivefold ministry doing the work of the ministry in the local church. Notice though in verse 32 of Numbers chapter 3, that Eleazar was appointed over the Gershons and Kohaths and in Numbers 4:33 the Merari's were under the direction of Ithamar. This represents the ranking of the apostles and prophets as first and second according to I Corinthians 12:28 and Ephesians 3:5. So now the leadership structure of the local church would look like this:

<pre>
                    God

        Apostle   Prophet

Evangelist Teacher   Pastor   Prophet   Apostle
</pre>

Again please understand that these all are meant to work together. All are necessary and vital to the spiritual health and maturity of believers. Now let me show you how these work in conjunction with the furniture in the tabernacle as well as God's command to Adam in the Garden of Eden.

The evangelist is the gift that gathers the sheep (people) that they might present themselves to

God as a living sacrifice on the brazen altar. The evangelist bringing people to the brazen altar as a living sacrifice is also a picture of being fruitful according to Genesis 1:28. "I assure you, most solemnly I tell you, Unless a grain of wheat falls into the earth and dies, it remains [just one grain; it never becomes more but lives] by itself alone. But if it dies, it produces many others and yields a rich harvest" (John 12:24 AMP). The animals were sacrificed at the brazen altar wholly in place of the people for their sins. Jesus says "Then he said to them all: "If anyone would come after me, he must deny himself and take up his cross daily and follow me" (Luke 9:23 NIV). The evangelist is the one gifted to bring people to repentance and being born again. God understands that death is what makes the seed available for planting in order to produce more fruit. As I mentioned earlier, the born again process is a spiritual process equal to Jesus' death, burial, and resurrection. The brazen altar is the place where we offer our bodies as living sacrifices to our God through repentance, baptism, and receiving the gift of the Holy Spirit. This is evangelism - bringing people to the born again experience, the cross.

The teacher represents the brazen laver. "I planted, Apollos watered, but God [all the while] was making it grow and [He] gave the increase. So neither he who plants is anything nor he who waters, but [only] God Who makes it grow and become greater. He who plants and he who waters are equal (one in aim, of the same importance and esteem), yet each shall receive his own reward (wages), according to his own labor. For we are fellow workmen (joint promoters, laborers together) with and for God; you are God's garden and vineyard and field under cultivation, [you are] God's building. According to the grace (the special endowment for my task) of God bestowed on me, like a skillful architect and master builder I laid [the] foundation, and now another [man] is building upon it. But let each [man] be careful how he builds upon it, for no other foundation can anyone lay than that which is [already] laid, which is Jesus Christ (the Messiah, the Anointed One) (I Corinthians 3:6-11 AMP). The brazen laver is where the priests would clean themselves with water from offering sacrifices and before they would go into the Tent of Meeting. "So that He might sanctify her, having cleansed her by the washing of water with the Word" (Ephesians 5:26 AMP). The teacher waters the seed with the word that it might grow and multiply. So in accordance with Genesis 1:28, the teacher has the responsibility of multiplication. "And he shall be like a tree firmly planted [and tended] by the streams of water, ready to bring forth its fruit in its season; its leaf also shall not fade or wither; and everything he does shall prosper [and come to maturity]" (Psalms 1:3 AMP). "'Your mother was like a vine in your vineyard planted by the water; it was fruitful and full of branches because of abundant water" (Ezekiel 19:10 NIV). The teacher is to grow the seed to maturity. Once the plant is grown to maturity, then and only then can it reproduce itself and multiply. The brazen laver represents cleansing and growing us to maturity through the washing of the word of God - making us ready for multiplication.

Now the pastor leads us into the Holy Place to the table of showbread. The pastor feeds the sheep, attends to their nourishment and needs, protects, and leads them in paths of righteousness. "Take heed therefore unto yourselves, and to all the flock, over the which the Holy Ghost hath made you overseers, to feed the church of God, which he hath purchased with his own blood" (Acts 20:28 KJV). The pastor also represents replenishing the earth in accordance with Genesis 1:28. The table of showbread was fresh manna that God would send down from heaven every day. The priests were to replenish the table every day. The manna was not to be kept and stored for God planned to give them fresh new manna every day. "Give us day by day our daily bread" (Luke 11:3 KJV). "After this the people gathered the food morning by morning, each family according to its need. And as the sun became hot, the flakes they had not picked up melted and disappeared" (Exodus 16:21 NLT). The pastor feeds the people. He doesn't store it for future use, but immediately distributes to each family, according its need. The pastor meets the needs of the people. Whether it is spiritual, physical, or mental, pastors meet the needs of the people. The bible speaks of replenish. The pastor replenishes the people. To replenish is to fill something again after it's been diminished or emptied. Once a child of God has been through the born again process, cleansed and grown to maturity, then he/she is sent out for multiplication. Now that child of God will need to be replenished of the nourishment they have poured out to others. This is where the pastor comes in. The pastor is also responsible for proper placement - leading the sheep beside still waters and making sure the sheep are always in an environment that will produce growth and multiplication.

The prophet speaks the direction and instruction of the Lord representing the golden candlesticks. "Thy word is a lamp unto my feet, and a light unto my path" (Psalms 119:105 KJV). "And we have the word of the prophets made more certain, and you will do well to pay attention to it, as to a light shining in a dark place, until the day dawns and the morning star rises in your hearts" (II Peter 1:19 NIV). The children of Israel subdued and defeated Jericho by the direction and instruction of God. Isaiah prophecies, "This is what the LORD says to his anointed, to Cyrus, whose right hand I take hold of to subdue nations before him and to strip kings of their armor, to open doors before him so that gates will not be shut:" (Isaiah 45:1). Jeremiah prophesies, "You are my war club, my weapon for battle--with you I shatter nations, with you I destroy kingdoms," (Jeremiah 51:20 NIV). Micah prophecies "Rise and thresh, O Daughter of Zion, for I will give you horns of iron; I will give you hoofs of bronze and you will break to pieces many nations." You will devote their ill-gotten gains to the LORD, their wealth to the Lord of all the earth" (Micah 4:13 NIV). The prophet declares war on the territory that is to be subdued. No war starts without a declaration of war.

The Apostle lays foundation and sets up the kingdom as well as sends more for kingdom advancement representing the altar of incense. After Jesus had ascended up and was seated at the right hand of the father, he sends the comforter (the Holy Spirit) to further the kingdom. "While they were worshiping the Lord and fasting, the Holy Spirit said, Separate now for Me Barnabas and Saul for the work to which I have called them" (Acts 13:2 AMP). The apostle represents having dominion in accordance with Genesis 1:28. Dominion speaks of setting up government and settlements. Many don't believe in the ministry of apostles and prophets today, but I would like to make an argument for them. If God's intent is for the body of Christ to conduct itself as a kingdom, then, as explained before, every local church should be built on the foundation of the apostles and prophets. Apostles and prophets are not laying a different foundation then what was made before by Paul and the biblical apostles. But with every new colony (local church) the foundation must be made so that structure, economics, culture and all other things that are vital to the success of that colony can be established. The apostles are those gifted to establish and maintain it. In the Bible, many times we find Paul writing to churches, laying more foundation, correcting, exhorting, etc. So, apostles are not just needed for the foundation but also for maintenance and longevity. Apostles keep the church on task and in order with the master's plan. If we are ever to accomplish the goal of perfecting the saints for the work of the ministry, until we all come into the unity of the faith, we need holy apostles to take territory and establish a strong foundation as directed by the Holy Spirit.

I pray this book enlightens the body of Christ - not to go to another extreme, but to make the necessary adjustments to line up with God's will for His body and to give God's people the best leadership we possibly can.

11

WISDOM FOR GOVERNING THE FIVEFOLD MINISTRY

Many are afraid to move to this model of church government because they fear that order will be lost. They fear that if they let others operate then it will take away from them. They fear church splits, disobedience, and rebellion. But isn't the church experiencing these already even now? I want to show you how to prevent many of these things from happening using the fivefold ministry model.

The first thing we must understand is that there are three sets of gifts in the bible. Man's (natural) gifts according to Romans 12. Then the Holy Spirit's gifts according to 1 Corinthians 12. And the church's gifts according to Ephesians 4. One of the major issues in the church today is that many in the church are ignorant of what real authentic ministry is. And we have a flawed view of the anointing. Listen the anointing doesn't come just to make you feel good, it comes with power. We've got to learn to separate feel good ministry from power ministry. Both are needed, yet one provides temporary relief and the other permanent relief. Many times, feel good ministry was used to gain access for power ministry. I believe the church has settled for feel good ministry and not enough power ministry. The bible says that these signs will follow them that believe, they will cast out devils, speak with new tongues, lay hands on the sick and the sick will recover. Now that's power ministry and you don't have to have a title to operate in the power of God. It is here that Apostolic government is important. When a believer begins to operate in ministry most are only operating in their natural gifts. Many are traveling the country and even internationally using their gifts in their own strength. It was never meant to be this way. In Matthew 10 the first thing Jesus did was give them power. If our natural abilities were enough, he would have no need to give us power. What God wants to do is take our natural ability and combine it with his power to break yokes, set captives free, and transform lives. So how do we govern the gifts in the local church? We've got to separate them in levels. Those who are operating in their natural gifts according to Romans 12, should be labeled as beginners. Let's look at what Romans 12:6-8 says "We have different gifts, according to the grace given to each of us. If your gift is prophesying, then prophesy in accordance with your faith; if it is serving, then serve; if it is teaching, then teach; if it is to encourage, then give encouragement; if it is giving, then give generously; if it is to lead, do it diligently; if it is to show mercy, do it cheerfully."

At this level we are developing in character to include the ability to be on time, be prepared, depended on, and motives for ministry. Sadly, many don't pass the tests of this level and forfeit promotion. So many of our gifted people just don't value good character and excellence in ministry. It is when we as leaders begin to demand these things regardless of the level of natural gifting they have that our gifted people begin to take ministry to another level. Like musicians and singers who sing for salary but can't stay throughout the whole service. And if they do, they go into the lobby and don't pay the word being preached any attention. As leaders we can't play favorites regardless of the gifting level. Many are excellent on stage but can't operate in excellence off stage. Being late is not excellence. Leaving the service right after their performance, is not excellence. Excellence at the lowest level will produce excellence at the highest level. I'm not minimizing the importance of our natural gifts and how God is able to use them for his glory. But it is only the beginners level. There is more. We must realize that our singing, dancing, preaching, and teaching can all be done without the Holy Ghost.

The next level of ministry is when the Holy Spirit begins to cooperate with a person as they operate in their natural gifts. Making their ministry supernatural. As a young minister begins to minister with what God has given him/her according to Romans 12 we ought to encourage them to be open to the Holy Spirit cooperating with them and manifesting himself through them with the gifts of the Spirit. This is the second level of ministry. What an experience to see the Holy Spirit manifest himself in a word of knowledge, gift of tongues, miracles, or any other gifts listed in 1 Corinthians 12.

1 Corinthians 12:7 says "But the manifestation of the Spirit is given to every man to profit withal." This is clear intent that the manifestation of the Spirit is for every man. The gifts of the Spirit are

not just for elite persons whom God selects as he wills. No, the manifestation of the Spirit is for every believer. I believe that every believer should experience the manifestation of Spirit, not just certain ones. Especially those who claim to be called by God to leadership in ministry. Operating in spiritual gifts brings supernatural results. Even Jesus needed spiritual gifts to get the results he got. True ministry is displaying love and leadership through dependency on the Holy Spirit. This is the example of Jesus. If we attempt to do ministry solely based in our natural abilities, we will grossly fail to get the kind of real results that Jesus and the apostles were able to get. We can no longer settle for ministry that comforts and encourages only. We must operate supernaturally with the power of the Holy Spirit. When a believer has begun to see the manifestation of the Spirit cooperating with them, they will see supernatural results take place in their ministry. Learning to depend and cooperate with the Holy Spirit is the second level of ministry. This level will prove itself with supernatural results. Healing, deliverance, miracles, great faith, etc., are all manifestations of the Holy Spirit cooperating with a believer for ministry sake. It is at this level that a believer will find their specialty. Many times the Holy Spirit will operate consistently in a particular manifestation of the Spirit. The believer will begin to specialize in this type of ministry. This specialty is critical because it will play a vital role in support of the assignment God will give. Leaders should monitor the proficiency of the believers in the gifts of the Spirit before releasing them to itinerant ministry. Otherwise you're releasing a minister who is only ministering out of their own strength. Proficiency in the gifts of the Spirit is vital to believers. The third level of ministry is when God gives you an assignment according to Ephesians 4. Ephesians 4 gives us the five functions in which we as believers can function in advancing the kingdom. Evangelists function as the marketing and recruiting department. Teachers function as the training department. Pastors function in the supervisory capacity. Prophets function as advisors. And Apostles function as administrators. Now again because Ephesians 4 says "And he gave SOME, apostles; and SOME, prophets; and SOME, evangelists; and SOME, pastors and teachers," we believe that their should be more than just one of each in a local church. I actually believe that these serve as departments in which every believer can fit their ministry under a specific function. Even if they are still at the first level of ministry and really don't know exactly what God has called them to do. They can operate in that department that they believe their natural gifts best fit. A car salesman would be great working in the evangelism department. Of course a school teacher could work in the teaching department. A nurse would fit really nicely in the pastoral department. A consultant in the prophetic department. And of course a human resource administrator in the apostolic department. Now I know there is much more to these functions than just being able to function in that capacity, but the point is that these provide every believer a place to do the work of the ministry regardless of what level they may be on. But when a believer gets called to one of these functions, that calling comes with a specific assignment and the grace to teach and equip others. This believer must not only be proficient in the function but also in the gifts of the Spirit. They should be considered an expert in this area of function. Let's look at two examples. The first is Moses. Moses was a Prophet sent to Pharaoh to declare the word of the Lord and in leading the children of Israel into the promised land. He was a Prophet with the assignment of deliverance. Moses assignment was to deliver the children of Israel out of Egypt and into the promised land. He was proficient in the spiritual gift of working miracles. Without the proficiency in working miracles Moses would have been in uncharted waters. Moses had to rely on that gift quite often during his time as the deliverer and leader of the children of Israel.

Paul was an Apostle sent primarily to the Gentiles. He was an Apostle with the assignment of unity and equal rights between Jews and Gentiles. Paul was very proficient in the spiritual gift of the word of knowledge and functioned as an Apostle dealing mainly with order and doctrine.

This is why we need levels to ministry so that a believer can be fully equipped and efficient in their calling for maximum effectiveness. Senior leaders should establish these levels of ministry in their churches to help believers develop properly before being sent out to the masses. Senior leaders should want those that come from their leadership to represent them in the most excellent way. They should want those that they serve to produce results - not just entertainment.

Understanding that we now live in a superstar culture as it relates to ministry, everybody is trying to be latest and greatest to hit the scene. Many have business cards two weeks after they realize that ministry is an option for them. Youthful zeal can be both good and bad. But if not properly cultivated, it can take a believer down a dangerous path. This is why we must properly disciple young ministers but not in a way that imprisons them to just sitting and watching. I remember when the older saints would say, "you ain't ready". But they could never tell you what you needed to work on to get ready. Neither were they willing to work with you to get ready. Those days are over. Young people are refusing to be held in a prison. They need to be discipled and mentored properly. And if all believers are to do the work of the ministry then there is absolutely no way the Senior leader can disciple and mentor everyone by him/herself. We've got to develop teams and mature others so that we can get the maximum participation needed out of our fellow believers. The fivefold ministry, and the Tabernacle are two biblical examples of how God would have the church to be governed. I just don't understand why many in the church, especially those who claim to be apostolic, are using restrictive and bondage forms of church government. We should be looking for ways to get all believers involved in the work of the ministry. Senior leaders should be creating ways to get more people doing the work of the ministry.

We need reformation and we need it now. We've got to destroy the works of Constantine, the Catholic church, and this prison system form of government that the church has been using. Let's get back to the book, back to God's way and his plan to be fruitful, multiply, replenish the earth, subdue, and have dominion. The fivefold ministry and team ministry is that plan.

REFERENCES

Goll, Jim, The Coming Prophetic Revolution, Chosen Books: Grand Rapids, MI 2001

Terrell, Kim, The Call of a Prophet, Class at the Forerunner School of Prayer in Kansas City, Fall Trimester 2002

Steven Lambert, The Prophetic gift and offices, Real Truth Publications, Jupiter, FL 2001

ABOUT THE AUTHOR

An apostle, teacher, preacher, community activist, and gifted leader. Terry Stephens II is the founder and Sr. Apostle of Manifestation Church, formerly known as Truth & Wholeness Ministries. He is also the founder and CEO of Dad Leadership Group, a coaching and consulting firm teaching leadership through concepts of Discipline and Direction. He has served in ministry and leadership for many years and in many places throughout the country and abroad. He is also a proud Soldier in the United States Army. Apostle Stephens has a passion for leadership and ministry that brings growth and development to those he serves and is committed to bringing to the body of Christ, excellence in leadership.

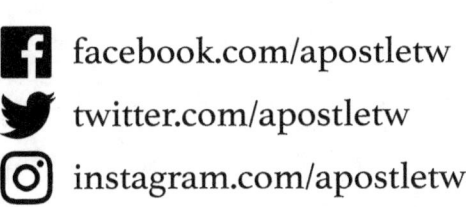

www.ingramcontent.com/pod-product-compliance
Lightning Source LLC
Chambersburg PA
CBHW072046290426
44110CB00014B/1577